ALLEN PARK PUBLIC LIBRARY #4
8100 Allen Road
Allen Park, MI 48101-1708
313-381-2425

S0-BJM-883

ALLEN PARK PUBLIC LIBRARY #4
8100 Allen Road
AllenPark, MI 48101-1708
313-381-2425

http://www.allen-park.lib.mi.us

DISCARD

J 394.266 W (P/T)

Christmas in
HOLLAND

A rink on the Museumplein (Museum Square) in Amsterdam attracts skaters of all ages during the holidays. One of four museums on the square, the Rijksmuseum (above) is home to a major collection of Dutch masters.

Christmas in HOLLAND

Christmas Around the World
From World Book

World Book, Inc.
a Scott Fetzer company
Chicago

Staff

Executive Committee

President
Donald D. Keller

Vice President and Editor in Chief
Paul A. Kobasa

Vice President, Marketing & Digital Development
Sean Klunder

Vice President, International
Richard Flower

Controller
Yan Chen

Director, Human Resources
Bev Ecker

Marketing

Director, Direct Marketing
Mark R. Willy

Marketing Analyst
Zofia Kulik

Editorial

Associate Director, Supplementary Publications
Scott Thomas

Managing Editor, Supplementary Publications
Barbara A. Mayes

Senior Editor
Kristina Vaicikonis

Researcher
Annie Brodsky

Administrative Assistant
Ethel Matthews

Manager, Contracts & Compliance (Rights & Permissions)
Loranne K. Shields

Editorial Administration

Director, Systems and Projects
Tony Tills

Senior Manager, Publishing Operations
Timothy Falk

Associate Manager, Publishing Operations
Audrey Casey

Manufacturing/Production/ Graphics and Design

Director
Carma Fazio

Manufacturing Manager
Barbara Podczerwinski

Production/Technology Manager
Anne Fritzinger

Production Specialist
Curley Hunter

Proofreader
Emilie Schrage

Manager, Graphics and Design
Tom Evans

Coordinator, Design Development and Production
Brenda B. Tropinski

Contributing Photographs Editor
Clover Morell

Manager, Cartographic Services
Wayne K. Pichler

© 2011 World Book, Inc. All rights reserved. This volume may not be reproduced in whole or in part in any form without prior written permission from the publisher. For information about other World Book publications, visit our website at www.worldbook.com or call 1-800-WORLDBK (967-5325). For information about sales to schools and libraries, call 1-800-975-3250 (United States) or 1-800-837-5365 (Canada).

Library of Congress Cataloging-in-Publication Data
Christmas in Holland
     p. cm.-- (Christmas around the world)
   Summary: "Customs and traditions of the Christmas holidays as celebrated in Holland and other provinces of the Netherlands. Includes crafts, recipes, and carols"-- Provided by publisher.
   ISBN 978-0-7166-0821-9
   1. Christmas--Holland. 2. Holland--Social life and customs.
I. World Book, Inc.
GT4987.54.C47 2011
394.266309492--dc23

2011023131

Printed in China by Shenzhen Donnelley Printing Co., Ltd.
Guangdong Province
1st printing September 2011

World Book, Inc.
233 N. Michigan Ave.
Chicago, IL 60601

The editors wish to thank the staff of the Netherlands Consulate-General at Chicago for their assistance in this project. For research and translation assistance, we thank Edmée Pratt-de Ruyter de Wildt and Louisa M. Ruyter. We would also like to thank the Gehring family for their generous help in answering our many questions.

The story "The Three Skaters" (pp. 40-42) and the St. Nicholas songs (pp. 74-77) are adapted from Santa Claus, The Dutch Way (The Hague: Albani), with the permission of the Ministry of Foreign Affairs, The Hague.

"A Little Child Is Born" ("Er Is een Kindeke Geboren," pp. 78-79) is adapted from "De Nederige Geboorte" ("The Simple Birth"), arranged by Walter Ehret, words adapted from a Flemish/English translation by George K. Evans. From THE INTERNATIONAL BOOK OF CHRISTMAS CAROLS, copyright © 1963, 1980 by Walter Ehret and George K. Evans. © Walton Music Corp. Used by permission.

ALLEN PARK PUBLIC LIBRARY #4
8100 Allen Road
Allen Park, MI 48101-1708
313-381-2425

Tiny lights twinkle on trees lining a canal in Amsterdam as the city prepares for Christmas. ▶

Contents

SPANJE

Saint Nicholas—or Sinterklaas, as he is called
in the Netherlands—arrives in Amsterdam aboard his ship,
the Spanje, as throngs of children gather
in the harbor to greet him.

A Sinterklaas Parade

Sinterklaas! The very word fills every Dutch child with joyful anticipation, as the days grow shorter and frost begins to etch the windowpanes. Mystery and magic, a spirit of goodness, and light-hearted merriment all surround the image of this white-bearded, robe-bedecked visitor. All year long, Dutch children eagerly await his appearance. Finally, St. Nicholas, as Sinterklaas is also known, arrives well before his feast day of December 6.

Mid-November finds his steamer chugging through the canals of North Holland, South Holland, and the other provinces of the Netherlands. (Many people also use Holland as an informal name for all of the Netherlands.) Also aboard the ship is the saint's faithful servant, Zwarte Piet—Black Pete. Some people say that Zwarte Piet is dark-skinned from climbing down chimneys to deliver Sinterklaas's gifts. Others say that he is a Moor, a descendant of people from northwestern Africa who conquered Spain in the 700's. A fully costumed crew that often includes hundreds of Petes and the saint's famous white horse, Amerigo, complete the group. They are said to have journeyed all the way from Spain to prepare for St. Nicholas Eve. Called Sinterklaas-avond, it is one of the most special nights of the year for the Dutch.

Traditionally, Amsterdam always hosted the saint's official entrance into the country. However, in modern times, Sinterklaas chooses a different city each year for his first appearance of the season. He arrives aboard the steamer Spanje, the Dutch word for Spain. Television cameras record the exciting event for the nation to view. But Sinterklaas also appears in other towns and villages throughout the country. He might dock in several places with the Spanje or travel on almost any other kind of boat. He also might arrive by helicopter, carriage, or bicycle—even by taxi. On this day, he is everywhere at once. He will continue to pop up through late in the day on December 5.

In Amsterdam, excitement fills the harbor as the steamer carrying Sinterklaas approaches. And the arrival of fun-loving Pete electrifies the celebration even more. Throngs of people gather to greet the famous visitors, waving flags, shouting, and singing a traditional song:

Look, there is the steamer from faraway lands.
It brings us St. Nich'las, he's waving his hands.
His horse is aprancing on deck, up and down,
The banners are waving in village and town.

Sinterklaas, accompanied by his helper, Zwarte Piet (Black Pete), enters the harbor in Amsterdam (right), in mid-November.

The steamer finally docks amid booming guns, ringing church bells, and cheering voices. The entire population of Amsterdam seems to have turned out for the occasion. Young and old, people of all different nationalities and creeds are celebrating. The event is without religious overtones, even though Sinterklaas wears the vestments of a bishop. Over the ages, he has become a universally beloved figure. Everyone is pleased to welcome the saint to the Netherlands.

The beloved saint greets the crowd as his helpers unload gifts that Sinterklaas will distribute to the children on December 5, St. Nicholas Eve.

Along the canals

Each year, the celebration seems to grow more and more elaborate. Today in Amsterdam, Sinterklaas's arrival includes a parade through the canals as well as one that winds through the streets. Floats and boats start out at the Maritime Museum in a long line that stretches for nearly a mile (1.6 kilometers) as it follows Sinterklaas's craft. They sail down the Amstel River, past the Nieuwe Amstel Bridge, the Toronto Bridge, and the Skinny Bridge. Then they turn into the Nieuwe Herengracht Canal and circle back around to the museum. All along the way, people crowd the bridges and shores, eager to wave at Sinterklaas and his crew as they float by.

When Sinterklaas and Pete finally disembark, the contrast between them is obvious. The saint is stately in bearing. He has a beard and is dressed elegantly in a bishop's white robe, crimson mantle, and tall red mitre headdress. His gloved hands are often adorned with

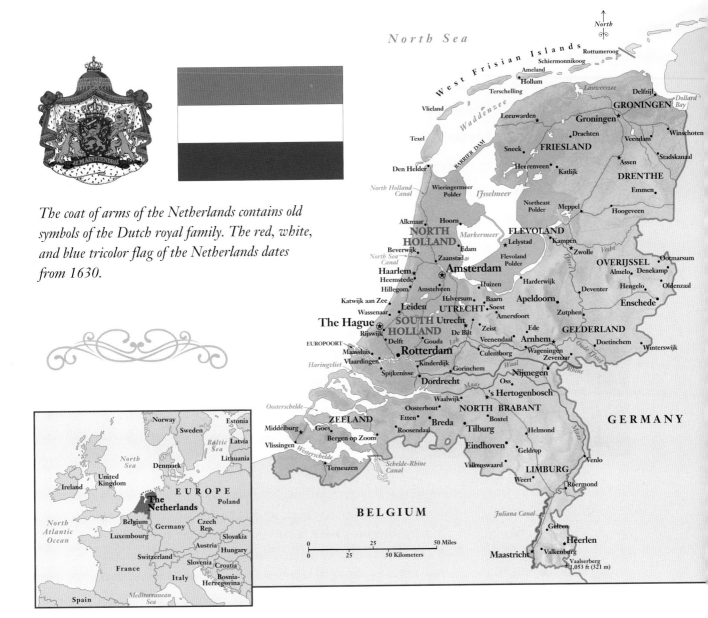

The coat of arms of the Netherlands contains old symbols of the Dutch royal family. The red, white, and blue tricolor flag of the Netherlands dates from 1630.

jeweled rings, and he always carries a golden crosier, or staff, shaped like a shepherd's crook, a symbol of his role as bishop.

Pete, on the other hand, is a mischievous, grinning character dressed somewhat like a 16th-century Spanish page. He paints a comical picture in his long stockings, short, puffed britches, tight-fitting jacket, pleated collar, and plumed Tudor bonnet (or Beefeater hat) tipped over one ear. All are in bright, contrasting colors. Many of the children in the crowd are wearing hats similar to Pete's—rakish berets in a variety of fabrics and colors.

Leading the parade

After the long-awaited pair alights from the steamer, Sinterklaas mounts his white horse, which is also elegantly adorned with trim of red and gold. On land, Sinterklaas always rides this magnificent steed. Youngsters believe Amerigo will carry Sinterklaas over the

The Netherlands is divided into 12 provinces, including North Holland and South Holland. The whole country is often informally called Holland.

The mayor of Amsterdam welcomes Sinterklaas to the city and offers him refreshments after his long journey from Spain. Sinterklaas's horse, Amerigo, is not forgotten—the tray also includes carrots for the steed.

rooftops each night until St. Nicholas Day, listening down the chimneys with Pete to check whether they are being good.

The youngsters have been waiting for what probably seems an eternity for this day to arrive. Many have, no doubt, coaxed their parents into bringing the entire family to the event. Assuredly, though, little prodding is required to convince any Dutch person to join the festivities. On occasion, there have been as many as three-quarters of a million people on hand in Amsterdam to greet Sinterklaas and Pete.

Traffic is usually in a complete snarl. *Trams* (streetcars that run on rails using electric power) come to a halt as passengers try to catch a glimpse of the celebrities and the ongoing activities.

The weather in the Netherlands at this time of year is generally cold, damp, and dreary. Rather than depressing the population, however, it seems to cheer everyone. These bleak conditions are often referred to as "real St. Nicholas weather." There is not a soul who would prefer any other weather for the occasion. In fact, some say the drearier the day, the more *gezellig* (warm and cozy) the atmosphere.

Dutch flags fly from houses all along the route of the saint's triumphant ride. In Amsterdam, the spectacle often begins at St. Nicolaaskerk, or St. Nicholas Church, near the central railway station. It leads to Dam Square in front of the Royal Palace.

The parade is an extravagant affair. There are balloons, brass bands, groups representing various children's organizations, acrobats and other entertainers, and dozens of floats. These often depict fairy-tale scenes from familiar stories or carry the newest popular cartoon characters.

During the parade, Pete is especially delightful. Often there is a whole brigade of Petes surrounding or following Sinterklaas. One year, there were more than 600! These playful figures might prance or dance along the parade route, telling jokes. "Petes" might also walk, cycle, zip around on rollerblades, or ride small motor scooters that make ridiculous noises.

No matter what they may be doing, the "Petes" are never far from the saint. Often, a group of them in their courtly costumes will run around with sacks, passing out marzipan and other candies to the youngsters in the crowd. Whatever the case, this collective Pete adds unbounded mirth to the event.

Welcoming Sinterklaas

In all the cities, towns, and villages in which Sinterklaas appears, local officials are always on hand during the celebration. The mayor and others in his group frequently dress formally for the occasion in top hats and tailcoats. They might welcome Sinterklaas the moment he arrives. They then enthusiastically join the parade, with St. Nicholas and his stallion in the lead. Often, a police motorcade and a big brass band will head them all. The route generally leads to a square adjacent to the town hall or to a large market place. There, the mayor greets Sinterklaas with an official welcome for all the gathered citizens to hear. In some years, Queen Beatrix, the ruling monarch of the Netherlands, and her children have attended the festivities in Amsterdam to add their greetings to the revered saint.

Also in Amsterdam, and elsewhere where the event is televised, a newscaster may corner Sinterklaas for an on-the-spot interview.

Children line the parade route through Amsterdam, eager to shake St. Nicholas's hand or to pat Amerigo as he goes by.

Whether watching in person or at home on their television sets, the little ones are always eager to hear what the saint has to say.

Meeting the saint

Then comes the time for the prestigious visitor to step to the podium and speak to those in the crowd. Sinterklaas usually begins by thanking the officials and everyone else present for the warm welcome he and Pete have received. But he is brief with these comments. He is eager to address those most important spectators who have been waiting so long and patiently: the children. He tells

Sinterklaas always appears in his formal bishop's robe and crimson mantle and carries his staff, the symbol of his office.

them how happy he is to be back in the Netherlands after a year spent in Spain. Then he may review the type of behavior he expects from them in the coming days. Whatever his words, the little onces listen attentively. Some are lucky enough to perch on the shoulders of an adult, thus gaining a better view.

After his speech, Sinterklaas mingles with the crowd. He never hesitates to stop and grasp a small, outstretched hand along the way. Also customary from the good saint are whispered warnings into little ears about behaving during his stay. Sinterklaas may remind some children about their conduct records, which he has been keeping in his big, red book. He often reads from this carefully recorded log when out among his young followers. It reveals his detailed knowledge of their year's activities, both good and bad.

Some children are eager to rush to the saint for a short chat. Others are a bit dubious about making direct contact with the immortal character. Sinterklaas can overlook a little shyness, however. He is a kind and tolerant figure who, above all else, loves every child.

During his talks with the children, Sinterklaas might drop hints about the kind of snack his horse prefers. The youngsters are eager to hear such information. They will be leaving hay or carrots for Amerigo at night, in a shoe set near the hearth, in hopes of finding a treat from St. Nicholas the next morning. Dutch youngsters set out the snacks often during the evenings between the parade and December 5. The treats they receive in return, of course, depend upon their past record and current behavior, which Sinterklaas and Pete will watch closely.

Frivolous Pete and his treats

Although Pete is a marvelous character who thrills the children almost as much as Sinterklaas himself, he does so in a far different manner. Compared with the stately saint, Pete is quite the frivolous fellow, engaging in all kinds of antics. He jumps, hops, skips, and rolls his eyes to the children's delight.

Pete is known to carry with him one or more unique objects. The most important is the famous big red book in which Sinterklaas keeps a record of the children's behavior. Pete lets it be known that the saint keeps excellent track of each little one! After all, this is precisely what Pete helps him do all year long back home in Spain.

Pete might also carry a handful of birch rods or switches. It is said he uses these to punish naughty children. Although no one has ever seen him actually do so, the rumors continue to keep the children on their best behavior. Sometimes, as a warning, Pete leaves a rod or switch with the treats. Badly misbehaving children may receive no treats at all, only the rod or switch.

The third object that Pete carries is a large sack brimming with goodies. He tosses marzipan, chocolates, or other sweets to the children he meets. Some say this big bag, though delightful when full, is also large enough when empty to hold a naughty child of any size who needs to spend a year in Spain with Sinterklaas. Although some youngsters might question whether anyone ever suffers this punishment, all are unwilling to risk finding out.

Pete enjoys interacting with the children. Often, he will introduce a willing youngster to the famed Sinterklaas. Tots and teens alike delight in

Pete carries the big red book in which Sinterklaas records every child's behavior.

Children, wearing red mitres like the one Sinterklaas wears or colorful bonnets like Pete's, eagerly wait to receive the treats Pete has in his big sack.

A volunteer puts the finishing touches on her "Pete" costume as she prepares to join the parade.

his tricks and silly actions. Consequently, wherever Pete is found, there will inevitably be a group of young people surrounding him. They are all attentive, eager for fun, and hoping for a treat of some sort.

One of the delicious delights Pete is sure to carry in his sack is pepernoten. These are small, round, hard cookies flavored with spices of the season: cinnamon, nutmeg, anise, and cloves. The tasty nuggets are a regular sweet treat at St. Nicholas time. Pete would not think of traveling anywhere without an abundant supply.

The season of Sinterklaas

Before St. Nicholas's arrival and during his stay, the towns and cities of the Netherlands dedicate their decorations to Sinterklaas. Merchants launch advertising campaigns and special sales for St. Nicholas presents. Loudspeakers fill shopping malls with St. Nicholas songs. Such large towns as Amsterdam and The Hague have colored lights strung over the streets. These are suitable canopies for Sinterklaas parades. Later, when Sinterklaas departs, Christmas shoppers also enjoy them.

Small, doll-like figures of Sinterklaas and Pete can be seen in many displays, stirring anticipation among strolling shoppers. In such large Dutch department stores as De Bijenkorf in Amsterdam, large, almost life-sized Pete dolls may climb ropes in a typical Pete-like antic. They lead all the way up to the towering ceiling.

Along with bakeries and confectioneries, costume stores bustle with business during this season. Between the arrival of Sinterklaas and St. Nicholas Eve, people shop for the vestments the saint wears and for Pete's colorful outfit. In the interests of credibility, imitators of both these celebrities must dress appropriately at all times. Sinterklaas and Pete will pop up at supermarkets, department stores and malls, schools, hospitals, parties, and even in homes the night of December 5. The costume shops, therefore, are well stocked with robes, capes, headdresses, and other apparel for rent.

Some actors even train at a special center to portray the good saint properly at private parties and similar functions. The center provides important advice on saintly conduct. Careful instruction on costuming shows how to fasten wigs and beards. Woe to the Sinterklaas who loses his beard at an inopportune moment!

Because Sinterklaas is most imposing with a craggy face and a deep, resonant voice, women rarely play his part. They do, however, frequently portray Pete.

The light-hearted traditions of the Sinterklaas celebration might make one wonder how such playfulness ever became associated with a saint. Who is St. Nicholas and where did he come from?

The story of St. Nicholas

Some believe that Nicholas lived in Asia Minor—an area occupied by present-day Turkey—from A.D. 271 to approximately A.D. 340. When the young man's wealthy parents died in an epidemic, he traded his life of luxury for a life of doing good deeds. A gift giver from the start, he distributed all of his wealth to the poor, then devoted himself to prayer. Soon he was named as bishop of Myra, a city in what is now southwestern Turkey. With this appointment came the splendid robes that he still wears today. Because he was so young at the time of his appointment, he was often called "the boy bishop." His long life of extraordinary deeds had just begun.

St. Nicholas would eventually become the patron saint of children, sailors and fishers, travelers, merchants, the persecuted, the imprisoned, and the poor. Lawyers and chemists also adopted him as their patron. Eventually St. Nicholas became known worldwide. He became the patron saint of countless cities, including Amsterdam, and of whole nations, including Greece and Russia. Sailors in the Aegean Sea, which lies between Greece and Turkey, wished one another luck with the saying, "May St. Nicholas hold the tiller."

Although gift giving is a trait common enough among well-wishers, the idea of placing gifts in stockings and shoes originated with St. Nicholas. According to legend, an unfortunate man was so poor, his three daughters planned to sell themselves as slaves because they lacked the dowries they needed to marry. Nicholas dropped three bags of gold through their window one night, and the girls were saved. One of the bags landed in a stocking hung by the fireplace to dry, giving St. Nicholas his unique calling card. In this way, St. Nicholas earned the faith of hopeful children the world over.

There are many other legends about this kindly saint. He revived three boys that an evil innkeeper had murdered. He crumbled prison walls in answer to the prayers of the persecuted. He even persuaded sailors to give portions of the grain from their holds to feed the starving poor. Then he mysteriously refilled the holds. The saint also calmed stormy seas and restored the lives of those killed in shipwrecks. In Germany, St. Nicholas evolved into Father Christmas. Dutch immigrants brought the tradition of "the visit of Saint Nicholas" to America, where the Dutch word "Sinterklaas" became "Santa Claus."

At home in Holland

Despite his worldwide fame, St. Nicholas seems to be most at home in Holland. Perhaps his popularity grew because his protégés included children, sailors, and merchants—three especially important groups in Holland. In the 1100's and 1200's, the tiny region became the site of no fewer than 23 St. Nicholas churches. Some of these still stand today. As early as the 1300's,

A child dressed as Pete clutches a treat from the Saint's helper as she watches the parade from a special perch.

choirboys of the churches were traditionally given the day off on December 6. They chose their own "boy bishop" to represent St. Nicholas and paraded through the streets begging for "bishop money." Half the funds went to the church and the rest, to the boys to spend on sweets.

By the 1600's, there were countless Dutch folk songs and legends about the saint, and famous painters drew subjects from his legends. Sweets called speculaas and taai-taai were associated especially with St. Nicholas. We know Jan Steen, a Dutch painter of the 1600's, enjoyed these because they appear in his painting called *The Feast of Saint Nicholas.* Perhaps other famous Dutch painters—Rembrandt, Frans Hals, and Jan Vermeer—enjoyed them, too.

Today, time has stripped away much of St. Nicholas's religious significance for the Dutch. Storytelling has relocated his home to Spain and given him Pete as a companion. Still, there is hardly another nation in the world that commemorates his feast day so widely and with

such enthusiasm. His memory simply delights the Dutch. His feast day brings forth glad hearts, good cheer, and the merriest celebration of the year.

Mystery and magic

As the festive St. Nicholas parade comes to an end, the weary but contented families return to their homes. Now the children's heads are filled with the mystery of the ingenious St. Nicholas and his wily friend, Pete. How did the two meet? Where will they live in the coming weeks? Once down the chimney, how does Pete climb up again, especially with a naughty child in his sack?

Everyone enjoys the day when Sinterklaas and Pete finally land in Holland.

While parents try to answer these baffling questions, Sinterklaas himself has but a fleeting moment to contemplate the season ahead. It will be a busy one for him and Pete. The two are well aware of the work cut out for them. There are schools to visit each day and children to check up on each night. There are records to keep and shoes to fill with goodies. Meanwhile, for the rest of the nation, the fun has just begun.

Shoppers explore a Christmas market beside the city Christmas tree in The Hague, the seat of the Netherlands government.

Saint Nicholas Eve

All Dutch children—and even those well beyond childhood—eagerly await St. Nicholas Eve. For this is the night of St. Nicholas's official visit to every Dutch home. The tradition of holding parties in his honor on this date stretches far back into the country's history. But before that magic night, many preparations must be made.

Dutch children know that Sinterklaas brings many of the delicious sweets of the season. But the marvelous Dutch bakers also lend a helping hand. The confectioners of the Netherlands rank among the finest in Europe, and they ably provide for the Dutch people, who are perhaps the greatest lovers of sweets. In early November, irresistible St. Nicholas goodies begin to appear in bakery shop windows. And in every home, the cooks, armed with beloved family recipes and special seasonal ingredients, set themselves at the oven.

Bakeries always offer a luscious display. One favorite Sinterklaas treat is called borstplaat. This hard, smooth fondant, or sugar candy, comes in many flavors, including vanilla, fruit, coffee, and chocolate. Generally, it is offered only once a year, especially for Sinterklaas-avond. Often prepared in heart-shaped molds, borstplaat also takes the form of squares, circles, or stars—all in various sizes and colors.

Almond-based confections are also immensely popular. Banketletters are flaky puff pastries filled with an almond paste and shaped into a letter, usually an initial. The letter M seems to be the most popular. Not only is it generally the heaviest, but it is also appropriate for all mothers. The Sinterklaas Eve party would be incomplete without a large pastry letter adorning the serving table.

Perhaps the outstanding confection of the holiday season, however, is the rich, almond-paste candy marzipan. Bakers have made marzipan since the 1400's. Until the early 1900's, however, it came only in simple shapes and was generally plain white. Today, the assortment of marzipan that fills confectioners' cases is staggering. Bakers present it in every imaginable shape and color, displaying their artistry as they please the eye as well as the taste buds.

The Dutch frequently special-order marzipan goodies as Sinterklaas gifts for friends and relatives. Often the selections have humorous

An elegantly decorated pastry called a banketletter is shaped into the letter S in honor of Sinterklaas.

Pastries of every imaginable kind fill the shelves of a Dutch bakery during the month before Christmas.

Smiling pink marzipan piglets make popular Sinterklaas gifts among family and friends.

meanings. Perhaps a marzipan tennis racket is appropriate for a cousin who loves to play the game but has not yet mastered it. A marzipan cell phone might go to a teenager who spends too much time texting. There are also figures depicting famous people, including Pete.

There are countless other marzipan items to be seen at the bakery, including marzipan versions of prepared foods of all sorts—hamburgers, hanging sausages, fried eggs, and bowls of the Dutch winter mainstay, pea soup. Dice and wooden shoes are old favorites, as are fruits, vegetables, and dairy products. These may be realistic-looking pieces resembling rounds of cheese, or comical ones decorated to look like dancing carrots. There are also innumerable animals. Pigs are a popular choice, perhaps as a reminder of the perils to the waistline when one eats too much marzipan! Often a bakery will have a life-sized marzipan piglet on display, from which shoppers may purchase a slice to take home.

The art of speculaas

Speculaas are another traditional treat during the Sinterklaas season. These are crisp spicy, brown-sugar cookies, somewhat like gingerbread. Speculaas come in many different shapes, including windmills, animals, hearts, people dressed in traditional Dutch costumes, and even St. Nicholas himself.

The term speculaas comes from the Latin word speculum, meaning "mirror." Traditionally, bakers pressed the dough for these cookies into carved wooden boards or planks. Each plank had a series of the same carving or any number of different ones. When the baker turned the cookies out onto a cookie sheet, the carved pictures appeared as mirror images, hence the name.

Carving these wooden molds of fruitwood and nutwood was once a baker's art. It required much skill, since the depth of each carving had to be the same all over for a cookie to brown evenly. Today, many of the original, hand-carved molds are valuable antiques and have become collectors' items. Many bakeries now make speculaas using a machine. Metal molds around the outside of a drum press the designs into the dough.

If a mold is unavailable, speculaas dough may be cut with a cookie cutter, rolled into cookie balls, or sliced into rounds or rectangles before baking. A more elaborate version calls for a filling of almond paste between two layers of speculaas dough. Cut into squares, these speculaas look somewhat like brownies.

Sometimes, bakers mold speculaas into large figures of men or women called "lovers" or speculaas-poppen—speculaas "dolls." Decorations for these cookies include white icing and almond halves. Some bakers like to sprinkle the cookie sheet with halved or slivered almonds before turning the molded cookies onto it. Whatever form speculaas take, these spicy cookies are a delight not to be missed.

Speculaas cookies were traditionally made in wooden molds carved by the bakers themselves. Today, many bakers use machines with metal molds.

More Christmas sweets

Another type of cookie, called taai-taai, also comes in "lovers" shapes, or taaipopjes. Although similar to speculaas, taai-taai cookies have a honey base. They are also thicker and chewier than the thin, crunchy speculaas. Taai-taai cookies come in human forms other than lovers and in animal shapes as well. The baker frequently sculpts one piece of dough at a time and finally assembles a true work of art. Taai-taai creations can be as long as 1 foot (30 centimeters) and often weigh as much as 1 pound (450 grams). Families eat them in several sittings, of course, so that everyone relishes the delectable flavor for days.

Large chocolate letters are also a specialty at this time of year. Chocolate is a particular favorite among the Dutch, regardless of its

Taai-taai cookies are honey-based and come in many different shapes.

Dutch girls mold their own favorite cookies, perhaps as a snack for Sinterklaas.

Borstplaat, a hard, smooth fondant (a sugar and water confection), is often made in heart-shaped molds and in various colors. Chocolate initials (bottom) are an eagerly awaited treat.

shape or the season it appears. But the chocolate Sinterklaas initials are an exceptional treat. They are available in plain or luxuriously fancy varieties of dark, white, or milk chocolate. Some are hand-decorated with swirls of light or dark chocolate frosting and sprinkled with nuts or other decorations. What a sweet dilemma, selecting just the right chocolate letter for a special gift! Sometimes, hosts use the chocolate letters as placecards, indicating each friend or family member's place around the St. Nicholas Eve table.

The Netherlands teems with other chocolate delights in these merry weeks. The sight of them fascinates children at shop windows. Wooden shoes filled with sweetmeats and small figures of Sinterklaas and Pete are just a few of the many items molded in all varieties of chocolate. Along with the treats come small, hollow staffs resembling the crosier St. Nicholas, as a bishop, carries with him. The staffs contain an assortment of chocolates and other candies.

Shoes before the hearth

Perhaps the only two people busier than the bakers at this time of year are the saint and his helper themselves. By night, they ride across the country's rooftops, listening through chimneys to learn which children deserve rewards for good behavior. On several of these

nights, youngsters place a shoe near the hearth, the kitchen stove, or almost any outlet giving access to where the two may alight. The shoes hold carrots, some hay, or other snacks for the saint's horse. Perhaps a dish of water will stand nearby as well, to quench the weary steed's thirst.

Pete, not Sinterklaas, descends the chimney or otherwise makes his way into the house to pick up the horse's snacks and leave goodies for the children. It would be a shame, after all, for Sinterklaas to soil his elegant robes. Pete also is the more agile of the two and always enjoys a good stretch and a steep climb.

There is no home to which Sinterklaas and Pete will come every night. They have too much ground to cover in three weeks to visit everyone each day. Also, parents are likely to remind their children that they must not be overly demanding. Sometimes, when the children put out their shoes, there will be no gifts to find in the morning.

In the past, Dutch children left wooden shoes by the hearth. Today, contemporary footwear has replaced wooden shoes both in everyday life and for St. Nicholas's visits. One custom is unchanging, however. Children who still believe often stand watch at night behind couches, chairs, or any other makeshift fortification. From there they hope to sneak a peak at Pete when he arrives in the darkness. The trick never seems to work. But no generation has become discouraged enough to give up the vigil whenever they can remain undetected—or so they think—by their parents.

A song for St. Nicholas

One method to entice Sinterklaas and Pete to a particular rooftop is singing. In the evening before going to bed, the children stand at the chimney and call to the saint with this favorite song:

A child has placed a shoe at the hearth with a carrot for Amerigo. Pete, in turn, has left a treat of pepernoten and a chocolate Sinterklaas.

> Nicholas, I beg of you,
> Drop into my little shoe,
> Something sweet or sweeter,
> Thank you, Saint and Peter.

In the morning, lucky children may find that their offering is gone. Some candy, a piece of fruit, or a small gift has taken its place. Often, a note is there as well, thanking the children for their thought-

A child shares a picture she drew with Sinterklaas as Pete looks on during a visit before St. Nicholas Eve.

fulness. It may also ask what they would like Sinterklaas to bring on December 5, when he makes his big visit with the best gifts. The youngsters, in turn, may respond the next evening with letters to the saint. The children often enclose a list of the items that they would most like him to bring on the big night.

Children's desires seem to be similar throughout much of the world. In the Netherlands, as in many countries, some of the gifts children request reflect current fads. Computer games and dress-up dolls are always popular items, as are books, trucks, and building sets.

Goodies that the children might find before St. Nicholas Eve include pink and white candy hearts with creamy fillings; a taai-taai, speculaas, or chocolate figure; some marzipan; and an orange or tangerine. Small gifts such as a yoyo, a tiny car, or a coloring book are common. There will also be pepernoten scattered over the hearth. Any of these might also appear on St. Nicholas Eve.

Anything the saint leaves delights the children. In the morning they sing thank-you songs up the chimney in hopes of another visit soon.

Early visits from Sinterklaas

Youngsters spend a portion of their time at home and at school drawing pictures of the friendly bishop and his jolly helper. This activity provides yet another way to win the saint's favor. Sometimes delightful and always endearing, the illustrations are hung near the fireplace. The children hope that the pictures will please Sinterklaas enough to persuade him to leave an extra treat.

Sinterklaas and Pete never content themselves only with nightly home visits. By day, they appear with gifts and treats at orphanages, hospitals, and homes for the aged. The pair often visits shopping malls and toy departments at local department stores, as well. There, Pete keeps an eye out for fun-loving adults who might be willing to join him in jest.

Of the sweets Sinterklaas and Pete distribute to the youngsters, speculaas are the favorite handout. Pete's pepernoten run a close second. Since they lack the richness of so many other holiday sweets, they are popular for nibbling. Because they are small and hard, they are easy to transport and almost impossible to break.

Schools are the most popular spot for personal visits from Sinterklaas and one or more "Petes." The students offer an exuberant welcome by singing a Sinterklaas song:

Good St. Nich'las is in Holland once again
With his horse and Peter from sunny Spain.
And even if he can't stay long,
We hope he'll stop to hear our song.
Dear St. Nicholas the door is open wide,
For you and Pete to step inside.
And we're singing, voices ringing, and our hearts rejoice
'Cause the saint loves all good girls and boys.

St. Nicholas is a good listener and greatly enjoys the entertainment the children provide. Pete, of course, has his sackful of goodies and gifts ready to go. He tosses pepernoten in great handfuls all over the classroom. The children dive to the ground, vying to claim the treats. Pete loves the confusion and urges the children on.

Sinterklaas may find that Pete has gone too far in his mischief. He scolds Pete in front of the children and orders him to another part of the room. After all, Pete has to behave, too!

Sinterklaas and Pete visit a school in Haarlem, in North Holland. Sinterklaas has brought some early gifts, and some of the children wear colorful bonnets similar to Pete's.

A splendid tree graces the interior of a department store in The Hague in the weeks before Christmas.

A little scolding never cools Pete's enthusiasm for fun. He performs humorous antics for the children's benefit as long as he and Sinterklaas are with them. Pete might hop onto tables and chairs or gleefully stuff a student volunteer into his sack—a warning to naughty children that they may be spending time in Spain this coming year.

The time arrives, however, to put all foolishness aside. A hush falls over the group as Sinterklaas opens his big red book. Pete stands nearby, a few birch rods in his hands. Gathered around the saint, the children listen carefully for their names. Does he know? Did he see? Of course, Sinterklaas knows everything!

The good saint might have some children come forward to sing a song. He may also question them about their behavior. Sinterklaas almost always presents the schoolchildren with some sort of surprise from Pete's large sack. Perhaps they will each receive a small gift. Before departing, he promises to visit their homes with gifts if they, in turn, promise to be good. Who could possibly refuse?

Toward the end of November, the glowing feeling of cheerfulness and fun mounts throughout the Netherlands. St. Nicholas Eve is rapidly approaching. The final preparations for the important evening are underway.

Preparing the surprises

The exchange of gifts among family and friends on December 5 is a unique event. The presents are not usually expensive or extravagant, nor are they beautifully wrapped. The tradition is, rather, to disguise or camouflage each present in an imaginative way. The creative wrapping is the gift's most important feature. Everyone calls the gifts "surprises."

A rhyme or poem always accompanies each surprise. Sometimes it expresses gratitude. More often, it humorously points out one of the recipient's quirks, foibles, or habits. Gentle teasing is this rhyme's goal. It is never meant to cause pain. Good-natured kidding is not only expected but applauded. The disguise and the verse, for example, might commemorate an incident or mishap of the past year. Although embarrassing at the time, it is now a source of joking. Sinterklaas himself signs these surprises and verses, so that the giver remains anonymous. In some areas, Pete signs his name, too.

The surprises of St. Nicholas Eve have given rise to the Dutch saying that best describes the Netherlands at this time of year. The entire nation "goes mysterious." For weeks, all have been shopping alone, secretly preparing surprises and frantically writing verses in isolated corners of the house. Sometimes family members lock themselves in their rooms for long stretches. They may shut doors in each other's face to ensure privacy and quiet while trying to compose clever rhymes. At work, no one is surprised to see an otherwise dignified colleague struggling to hide a package in something like a hollowed-out loaf of bread. Everyone knows one cannot take care of such a complicated task at home.

In the past, local department stores often provided help to those who felt incapable of writing their own poems. The stores employed a professional rhymester called a sneldichter. Sometimes with the aid of a rhyming dictionary, these speed poets could dash off a jingle in no time, all typed and ready for presentation. These days, some people turn to the Internet for help. For others, half the fun of the holiday lies in writing these playful rhymes on their own, regardless of their poetic quality. The more imperfect the verse, the more to laugh about.

Waiting for Sinterklaas-avond

St. Nicholas Eve is an exciting and busy day. Sinterklaas and Pete can still be spotted all over town as last-minute shoppers crowd the stores until closing. People clog the streets, attempting to get home from shopping in time to take care of final wrapping and make ready for the fun.

Shoppers search for the perfect gift at a Christmas market in Dam Square in central Amsterdam in December. The city's official Christmas tree stands before the Royal Palace.

Most Dutch people must go to work or school on St. Nicholas Eve. Students would naturally struggle to remain attentive to studies on this last day for impressing the saint. But teachers usually devote the morning to singing together, opening surprises, or just plain merrymaking.

An exchange of gifts between older students often occurs grab-bag style. An alternative is to draw names before December 5. Anonymous classmates can then match a surprise and poem to the recipients. They open the packages and read the verses one by one, to the hilarity of the rest of the class. Marzipan is a popular and inexpensive gift that lends itself well to humorous comments about classmates. The best present of all comes at noon, when the teacher dismisses class for the day.

Working adults are less lucky. They are often able to leave their jobs only in the late afternoon. Then they attend to last-minute details and hurry home to join in the festivities.

Evening draws near

The vigil of St. Nicholas is traditionally a time for family gatherings. The party itself is warm and merry, with parents and children sharing the fun. Many Dutch who find themselves away from home suffer

more nostalgia on this night than at any other time of year. In fact, young adults who work in other cities or countries have been known to request vacation time around St. Nicholas Eve—rather than Christmas itself—in order to be with their families.

After supper, the children begin listening for the tapping of St. Nicholas's horse on the roof. They may sing a song to help speed his arrival or pass the time trying to remember what they asked for on their lists to St. Nicholas. Someone, maybe Papa, remembers that he left something at the office. He rushes off, promising to be right back.

Everyone jumps when a loud knock comes at the door or a sharp tap sounds at the window. Mama opens the door a wee bit. There is Pete's hand! He flings fistfuls of candies and pepernoten into the hallway. This rain of goodies on St. Nicholas Eve night has given it a special name—strooiavond, or "scattering evening." The children throw themselves at the goodies, and then Pete is gone into the night. He has never shown his face. Only a bulging sack or basket of gifts remains on the doorstep.

There is a rumor that neighbors generally depend on one another for these mysterious deliveries. But there are no doubters in the

Winterland, a Christmas fair held in early December, fills Amsterdam's Rembrandt Square with shoppers, revelers, and even a Santa Claus figure—an unusual sight in Holland.

A family wraps the gifts they will present to each other on St. Nicholas Eve.

homes where Sinterklaas and Pete make personal appearances. The good bishop sits down in Papa's chair—Papa is still missing—opens his big book, and gently scolds each child about less than admirable traits. The children wonder, as usual, how he knows so much about them. None, however, would venture close enough to see whose handwriting is in the book, not even if they suspected their parents. Before departing, the saint may present each child with a gift. The youngsters know there are more to come.

There are two ways Sinterklaas gives the children the rest of their gifts this night. They may put their shoes near the chimney again, sing St. Nicholas songs, and go to bed. Then Sinterklaas and Pete drop the presents down the chimney into the shoes, as on previous nights. Elsewhere, Sinterklaas has already deposited the gifts somewhere in the house. The presents the saint gives the children right before he leaves may even contain directions on where to find the rest of them. If this is the case, the children head for the treasure spots.

When the children become older, their surprises join those of the grownups in a heap on the floor. The pile of packages is the source of another name for St. Nicholas Eve night. The Dutch call it pakjesavond, or "parcel evening." Each parcel carries the name of the person for whom it is intended.

The masters of surprises

The Dutch are said to be masters at surprise giving. Their imaginations never seem to run dry. Neither does their enthusiasm for creations other than their own. This must be why they love Sinterklaas so much. He made up all the surprises tonight. Look! He has signed every one.

The family takes turns unwrapping the surprises and reading the poems. All listen intently and relish the jokes and clever tricks. His originality knows no bounds. Mother, for example, may find a bracelet inside a raw potato dressed as a doll. But the potato could also be wrapped in tape, put into a milk carton, and placed in a bucket of ice along with a glass of cool refreshment. "Thank you, Sinterklaas!"

Mother says aloud, toasting with the official tribute to the saint. That toast will be made many times before the night is out.

Detailed treasure maps lead many on quests all over the house and even into the yard in order to find their surprises. Flower pots and mail boxes make excellent hiding places. The longer the discovery takes, the better a job Sinterklaas has done. So sometimes he confuses everyone by putting the wrong name on a package. Mother opens it, only to find a small box with father's name on it. Father opens the box to find a note sending his oldest son out the front door. There, on the step, is a molded chocolate figure. Ten minutes later, when the son breaks off a piece of the candy to eat, he discovers a note for his little sister. She follows directions, looks in the kitchen sink, and finds a picture book for her signed by the saint.

Sometimes the surprises are obviously a hoax—candies filled with mustard, crackers made of soap, or cookies with toothpaste icing. But everyone enjoys the inventive disguises and the dauntless labors Sinterklaas found time for again this year.

Some Dutch people take gift giving into their own hands on this night. They place surprises on other families' doorsteps, ring the bell, and run away as fast as they can. Sinterklaas never minds. Everything is still from him anyway.

The mysterious Frisian islands

Something, in the meantime, is wrong off the northern coast of Holland. The women and children of Ameland, one of the West Frisian islands, have disappeared! And so have the men. By dusk, only suspicious-looking strangers can be seen, scouring the streets, brandishing clubs, and blowing through buffalo horns that fill the silent landscape with an eerie din. Once again, Ameland, the "island of demons," is living up to its name. The baenfeijers are taking over.

These ghostly "street sweepers" are really the men in disguise. All 18 years and older, they are participating in a rite that is associated today with Sinterklaas but whose origins are lost in the area's pagan past. Their mission is twofold. They want to conceal their identity and sweep the streets clean of all the women—who, with the children, have taken refuge at home for the time being. Any

Mysterious men known as baenfeijers "sweep" the women and children off the streets until midnight on St. Nicholas Eve on the West Frisian Islands, off the northern coast of Holland. The reason behind the ancient pagan tradition is lost in time.

unfortunate female who ventures outside is asking for trouble. A baenfeijer will chase her, waving his club. She will have to jump over the club in a show of "submission." When the streets are finally empty, the baenfeijers, who are really advance troops, disappear. They are making way for another group of invaders.

The children, though cooped up for a time, have no reason to complain. Their huge festival for the season already took place on December 4. They wait with the others for the buffalo horns to sound again. Now the Omes are on their way.

Also called Sundeklazen, these are the men once again, in a complete change of costume. For weeks they have devised the ingenious, carnival-like dress. Restrictions lessen now, and the women and children are free to go outside—with an escort. They may visit one of the many open houses or inns, where the Omes flit about, speak mysteriously through their buffalo horns, and insist that women and girls dance with them. They may pound on the floor with their clubs to summon their chosen partners. Those watching try to guess the identity of the masked merrymakers, for the Omes change their costumes each year. Sometimes they even wear more than one costume a night.

Ameland is not the only place that is entertaining "guests" this evening. So are three neighboring West Frisian islands. Vlieland suffers an invasion of Sunderklazen; Terschelling, of Sundrams; and Schiermonnikoog, of Klozems. These are the local counterparts for Omes. Their missions are similar.

The villagers of each island dance and enjoy the revelry until midnight. In some places, the masks are cast aside when the clock strikes 12. The village of Hollum in Ameland, however, preserves this celebration in its purest form. Here, the Omes vanish into the darkness from which they came. They never reveal their identity, but, some say, they leave the women in charge again for another year.

In the rest of the country, families are beginning to relax. The children enjoy some sweets and one more drink of hot chocolate before going to bed, weary from the day's excitement.

The adults have their pastries and coffee, or perhaps some steamy bisschopswijn, or "bishop's wine." This delicious hot, spiced wine tops off the evening perfectly. The children are now dreaming of Sinterklaas, their beloved saint. He is on his way to a well-deserved rest in sunny Spain.

DELFT POTTERY

Not only is Holland famous for its chocolate, but it is also renowned for a distinctive blue and white pottery known as delft. The pottery is named for the town in which it originated.

Located in the province of South Holland, Delft produced blue and white tin-glazed earthenware that came to be called "delft." The pottery was especially popular from the mid-1600's to the mid-1700's. The term "delft" is also used to describe pottery made in England using a similar technique, as well as pottery made earlier in Delft that was painted in dark blue, orange, and green.

Dutch potters began to use the characteristic blue and white colors and to refine their designs after shipments of blue and white Ming porcelain reached the Netherlands in the 1600's. The Chinese pottery was of a higher quality than the original delft. It immediately became so popular that the Dutch potters realized they had to improve their wares to compete. The Dutch began producing plates, vases, wall tiles, and other decorative items to rival the Chinese products.

By the middle of the 1700's, the popularity of delftware had begun to diminish, and today, much of the pottery called delft is mass produced, primarily for the tourist trade. However, several factories in Delft still produce the high-quality, hand-painted pottery.

A selection of high quality Royal Delftware pottery is displayed in a shop in Delft, in the province of South Holland.

An artist paints an intricate design on a delft pottery vase with cobalt oxide. The black paint turns into the traditional delft blue color during the firing process.

ALLEN PARK PUBLIC LIBRARY #4

Candles glow in every window of the Gothic town hall and other buildings facing the historic market square of Gouda during the traditional kaarsjesnacht *(candle evening) in mid-December.*

Signs of Christmas

As the gaiety, fun, and surprises of Sinterklaas-avond fade away, calm and peace take their place. The Dutch prepare to welcome Christmas reverently, celebrating the holiday in a meaningful, religious way. Instead of lively parties, a spirit of good will and family togetherness dominate the second half of December. Christmas is "happy" more than "merry." There is less hectic rush, less hustle and bustle than in many other countries of the world.

This is not to say that there are no signs of Christmas in the stores, shopping malls, streets, and squares of the nation. To be sure, a great deal of activity—though muted in tone—is taking place.

Most towns have a majestic Christmas tree that stands, beautifully lighted, in the main square or market place. Amsterdam's tree is before the Royal Palace in Dam Square. To the north, in Groningen, a tall, dark green pine may tower over the Grote Markt.

In the historic town of Gouda in the province of South Holland, the Christmas tree-lighting ceremony in mid-December is a spectacular sight. This pageant, called kaarsjesnacht (candle evening) takes place in Gouda's market square in front of the beautiful Gothic town hall. The oldest in the country, the town hall dates from 1450. With little imagination, those who attend the opening ceremony find themselves back in the 1500's. No electric lights glare in any of the buildings facing the square. Instead, all the windows surrounding the square, and those of the town hall, shine with the soft glow of candlelight. The mayor throws the switch illuminating the huge evergreen, which overwhelms the scene. Carillons peal and a choir sings forth. Everyone in the crowd joins in, even foreign visitors who do not speak Dutch. These people sing along in their native languages, with the encouragement of their Dutch hosts.

People gather in buildings around the market square in Gouda, South Holland, to watch the lighting of the town's spectacular Christmas tree.

The cities prepare for Christmas

Municipal Christmas trees, and many others, often come from Norway, the source of some of the biggest and most beautiful evergreens in Europe. The Dutch also count on Finland, Germany, and Sweden for a great share of the Yuletide greenery that will adorn the flat landscape of the Netherlands.

The cities and towns sparkle with lights strung high above the streets and along bridges over the canals. Splashes of red and green cast a hazy glow from shop windows on misty evenings. Stores in large cities display bright decorations with Christmas trees, boughs of holly, and greenery in lush clusters.

Such large department stores as PC Hooftstraat and De Bijenkorf in Amsterdam are adorned in the traditional decorations of the season. Silver and gold garlands and boughs of evergreen hang elegantly above busy shoppers at counters filled with lovely merchandise. Many stores have a Christmas tree trimmed with lights and colored ornaments. Santa Claus decorations may be present in some places, showing the growing influence of the famous character on the Dutch Christmas season. (However, many traditionalists take exception to the introduction of this non-native character.) Colorful displays of Christmas and New Year's cards in Dutch and English are for sale in many stores and shops.

Table decorations for the Christmas feast and decor for other rooms in the home are an important part of the Dutch holiday and require careful planning. To help the host or hostess, flower markets have a magnificent selection from which to choose. Open stalls fill with buyers purchasing fresh flowers, greenery, and garnishes for decorating. There are evergreen wreaths, holly branches, and an occasional sprig of mistletoe. Greenery comes bunched in baskets or already grouped with fresh flowers and trimmed with a bow to make a festive wreath or centerpiece. Pine cones are loose or in pinecone wreaths.

Festive lights outline a bridge over one of Amsterdam's canals in the month before Christmas. Bicycles, a favorite form of transportation among the Dutch—even in wintertime—form a row on the street above.

Amsterdam's official Christmas tree lights up Dam Square as shoppers hurry past.

Tulips, chimes, and carillon bells

Bulb flowers, such as tulips and lilies, are especially popular at Christmastime. Stalks of pussy willows also provide attractive accents at home. Red and white poinsettia plants are also popular among the Dutch, who often call them Christmas roses. Lovely candle arrangements ringed with evergreens and fresh flowers catch everyone's eye.

Tulips are a popular flower among the Dutch at Christmastime and can be found in flower markets throughout the country.

Sometimes, the flower stalls are part of a Christmas market, which many Dutch towns and cities host during the month of December. A variety of booths offer such treasures as Christmas ornaments and handmade gifts. For those who become cold and hungry while shopping, other booths feature mulled wine, hot chocolate, and the traditional tiny Dutch pancakes called poffertjes. Some Christmas markets also include entertainment. At the market on the Museumplein (Museum Square) in Amsterdam, a huge ice skating rink tempts children and adults alike. A market during Christmas week in Rotterdam is both a gift mart and a fun fair that all enjoy.

To carry all their festive purchases home, many shoppers bring their bicycle—a common means of transportation for the Dutch. It is not an unusual sight to see someone pedaling home through the snow on a bike laden with packages.

Music is an essential part of the Yuletide season. The Dutch love to sing and listen to music of all types, and Christmas only whets the appetite for more. Chimes and carillons sound over and over. Amsterdam's Oude Kerk, or "Old Church," provides carillon concerts throughout the year. December finds entranced audiences enjoying them almost every afternoon. Many other churches and concert halls across the country also offer musical performances. The variety satisfies any preference.

Trimming the tree

The wonderful fragrance of fir and pine wafting from Christmas tree stands tempts buyers to examine the choices. In Amsterdam, the sale takes place on the Singel Canal. In the center of the old town, it is the city's innermost waterway. Beginning in mid-December, the bordering area closes off to traffic. Vendors unload all sizes of evergreens from flat-bottomed barges lined up along the water's edge. Holly branches and boughs and wreaths of fir and pine join the floating green display.

Trimming the Christmas tree is an activity for the whole family, from selecting ready-made decorations to creating them by hand. The large department stores in most major cities have special Christmas decoration markets. Children and adults enjoy browsing among the brilliantly colored tree bulbs, sparkling tinsel garlands, and other gleaming decorations on display. The family will perhaps choose some new items for this year's tree.

A widespread custom, especially among apartment dwellers, is to purchase a yellowish paper star studded with small holes through which the light from an electric or LED bulb gleams. These three-dimensional decorations, called Advent stars, shine in windows starting in early December. Their presence marks the time until Christmas. Hung in the windows of high-rise buildings, Advent stars reflect a glowing checkerboard of Christmas cheer.

Families in single-family houses sometimes decorate their garden trees and front doors with lights. Also common are frosty window-stars that families make with cutout star patterns and a can of artificial snow.

Getting the tree and all the other purchases home on a bike is no easy task, but it is a common sight in the weeks before Christmas.

Ornaments that Dutch families make at home have traditionally included small pinwheels made of colored foil and larger ones to adorn the treetop. Gilded, silvery, and many-colored walnuts may hang from the tree on thin wires secured within the nutshells. Bead garlands are easy to make and drape over the tree boughs. Such fruits as apples, oranges, and tangerines, though heavy, will also stay in their places with a little maneuvering and some string or wire. Pine cones are a versatile material with which the entire family may work—painting, glittering, and arranging in the perfect spot.

Vegetables add bright spots of color to fresh garland, while candles add a festive glow to every corner of the house.

The bakery also provides popular ornaments for the Dutch, who especially like to place edible decorations on their trees. How long these last, of course, depends on the children. Sugar bells and stars are favorites, as are various shapes of chocolates in foil wrappings. Kerstkransjes are small Christmas wreath cookies that are also easy to make at home. The family ties them to the tree with red ribbons.

In the past, small candles were the last ornament to go on the tree. Many Dutch families used only red or white candles in silver holders. Once lighted, this decoration demanded a constant vigil. (A bucket of water was often placed nearby in case of emergency.) When the rest of the room was darkened, the final effect of the illumined candles was an enchanting glow. It reflected the warmth and light of the true meaning of Christmas. Today, families in the Netherlands—as elsewhere throughout the world—use strands of electric lights to illuminate the tree, in the interest of safety.

On Christmas Eve, candles glow from the dining table, side tables, the mantel—almost anywhere. Garlands of evergreen branches, embellished with pine cones and even fruits and vegetables, might frame windows and doorways. Together, the fragrant candles and sweet-smelling boughs fill the house with quiet pleasure.

In Roman Catholic homes, there will probably be a kerststal, or crèche, near the Christmas tree. The children in these families enjoy setting the figures of the Nativity in just the proper arrangement. The crèches also appear in Catholic churches and chapels.

After a family shopping trip in the brisk December weather, the family may settle down before the Christmas tree. The children enjoy some hot chocolate and a warm batch of delicious sneeuwballen. These "snowballs" are deep-fried spoonfuls of cream puff dough dotted with candied fruit and currants or raisins. A good dusting of powdered sugar on top resembles snow. A special delight during the entire month of December, sneeuwballen are also a treat for New Year's Eve.

The Three Skaters

Anytime during the Christmas season, Dutch families enjoy Christmas stories. Reading aloud by the light of the Christmas tree is a time-honored custom. A favorite legend is that of "The Three Skaters":

> The canals stretched straight and frozen till they faded away in the distance. Gnarled old willows stood in ragged rows like worried onlookers. The year's harvest had been poor. Farmers wondered how they would manage to pull through the winter.
>
> One farmer skated home over the frozen canal. He had been to market that day. All he was able to get for his few pennies was a bagful of apples, now slung over his shoulder. He hurried along, thinking how disappointed the family would be with the meager results of his marketing, and Christmas so near.
>
> Then through the falling dusk appeared his neighbor, a miller. He carried a few loaves of bread the baker had given him in exchange for a sack of flour. The two skaters greeted each other without a word as they traveled on through the silent evening. Each sank into his own thoughts, knowing that the other man's were the same.
>
> Soon another neighbor joined them, this time a pig farmer. He carried a side of bacon for which he had found no buyer in town.
>
> The strong, regular strokes of the silent men's skates were the only sounds in the wide, wintry landscape. It was getting even colder now. The men huddled deeper into their woolen mufflers.
>
> The heavy clouds began to look strangely lit, as by an inner light. The skaters noticed the moon appearing from behind the clouds. One cold, stark beam pointed straight down to a decrepit, lonely barn across the snow-covered pasture on the left.

Suddenly a sound came from the barn, the sound of a baby crying. "Hey!" the miller called to his companions. "Stop!" The other two halted, annoyed with him. It was cold and late—time to be home.

"Listen!" said the miller, pointing his finger to the barn. There was no mistake. The others heard it, too. There was a baby crying there.

"But that barn's been empty for years," said the farmer.

"An old man keeps his sheep there," added the pig farmer, "but that's no bleating."

For a moment the three men hesitated. Then they removed their skates and crossed the pasture to investigate. As they approached the moonlit barn, the crying became quieter as a woman's gentle voice began to hum a soft lullaby. The neighbors were baffled. Then the miller moved forward and opened the door. Their eyes adjusted to the dim glow of the lantern inside. They saw that their ears had not deceived them.

A young woman they had never seen before sat on the cold floor. In her arms she held a newborn baby. Her coat was wrapped around the little boy, who was now sleeping peacefully. An old man was raking together some hay in a corner. Now the mother laid down her baby tenderly on that little heap of softness in the cold, rough barn.

"We come from far away," the old man began to explain, as if to

The centuries-old windmills of Kinderdijk, in South Holland, strung along a misty, frozen canal at dusk, set the scene for a favorite Dutch Christmas story, "The Three Skaters."

answer unspoken questions, "and we still have far to go. It was time for the wife to have the baby. We are grateful that we found this barn. But we can't stay long, for we have no food and no firewood. We shall have to move on tomorrow."

The three men just stood for a moment, unable to speak. Then, driven as by one force, each lowered the sack from his shoulder and emptied it in front of the young mother. The apples, the bread, and the bacon gleamed curiously in the flickering lantern light. Her eyes shone with peace and quiet acceptance. They felt a sense of well-being so strong that they were puzzled. One by one they took a shy look at the dozing infant, gathered their empty sacks, and turned to leave. Gently they closed the door behind them.

Back at the canal, they tied on their skates, swung the sacks over their shoulders, and started on the last stretch home. They all wondered about the little scene they had just taken part in. Strangely, none was worried about coming home empty-handed. They felt almost light-hearted in the cold, frosty night.

The sacks they carried soon seemed to be getting heavy. By the time they reached the village, the three skaters almost bent double under the load. Why, they could not explain.

At the church, the three men parted. The last few steps home seemed almost unbearable, so heavy was the weight on their shoulders. They opened their back doors and stepped inside. They dumped the sacks on the floor and looked at the expectant faces around the fireplace.

"Father is home!" The youngsters jumped up and began to tug at the sacks. They pushed, laughed, and romped, as if they had discovered a new kind of game.

When the men finally opened the sacks and turned them out over the kitchen floors, food of all sorts rolled across the neatly scrubbed tiles. There was candy for the children, Dutch honey cake for the mothers, and fruits for the fathers. What happy feasts they had that evening in all three homes!

When there was quiet again, the three men sat contentedly, each at his fireplace. But in spirit they were far away. Their thoughts hovered around a moonlit barn, around a simple, lanternlit scene, where a miracle had come to pass.

The Christmas story ends and bedtime is near. The children help blow out the candles on the mantle and table, marking the end of another evening. Kerstmis, the tranquil Christmas celebration, is one day closer.

DUTCH CHEESES

The Dutch are world-famous for their cheeses. Over centuries, Dutch farmers built dikes and drained soil that was once covered by swamps or lakes to make fertile green pastures for herds of dairy cows. These herds produce enough milk to make the Netherlands one of the leading cheese-producing nations of the world.

The Dutch have become particularly renowned for several different kinds of cheese, some of which are associated with towns and markets that bear their name. Today, cheese markets in the towns of Alkmaar, Gouda, Edam, and Hoorn operate just as they did in the Middle Ages. Visitors can watch as kaasdragers (cheese porters) dressed in traditional garb carry huge wheels of cheese on stretchers to the weighing house. There, merchants sample the cheese and agree on the price it should bring. The taste of a particular cheese—and also its price—depends, in part, on its age.

Gouda for example, is generally a mild, semi-hard cheese made from whole milk. It can be made from cow's, sheep's, or goat's milk. As it ages, it becomes harder in texture, darker in color, and more intense in flavor. It is generally dipped in red or yellow wax for a younger cheese and black wax for an older one.

Edam cheese is also mild. It has a lower fat content than Gouda and is coated in red wax. Edam, too, becomes harder and more intense in flavor as it ages.

Many Dutch families eat cheese twice a day, at breakfast and at lunch, often as part of a sandwich.

Wheels of cheese are stacked at the cheese market in Alkmaar, in North Holland. Kaasdragers (cheese porters) carry the cheese to the weighing house, where merchants sample and price it.

Families take to the ice during the Christmas holidays.

Two Christmas Days

Dutch families celebrate not one, but two Christmas days. December 25 is Eerste Kerstdag, or First Christmas Day. Tweede Kerstdag, or Second Christmas Day, follows on December 26. Although the Dutch observe these two holidays somewhat differently, they devote both to faith and family.

There is, of course, only one Christmas Eve. When it falls on a workday, some people may be able to leave work in the afternoon, providing extra time to shop for groceries for the Christmas feast the next day. Others will take the opportunity to visit with relatives. In the evening, many families attend church services, beginning the religious observance that characterizes First Christmas Day.

Christmas morning finds many families going to worship. They wish one another "Vrolijk Kerstfeest," "Merry Christmas," as they meet. Most churches welcome their congregations with Christmas trees and festively decorated altars. Evergreens and fresh flowers enhance the special services. So do the inspiring voices of the choirs.

Hearts are filled with good will and thanksgiving as families return home for koffietafel late Christmas morning. This meal is not breakfast, which took place before the trip to church. It is, rather, an elaborate brunch. The meal is called "coffee table" because coffee is usually served.

Koffietafel may include such luxury foods as smoked salmon or pate. It also usually features kerstkrans. Kerstkrans is similar to the banketletter pastry served at St. Nicholas time. However, for the first day of Christmas, it is shaped like a large wreath and decorated with lemon icing, candied fruit, holly, and a big red bow. Kerstkrans is heavy and rich and quite suitable for serving as a dessert.

In some areas of the country, such as the large cities of North and South Holland, the exchange of gifts at Christmas has become popular and may take place on the morning of Eerste Kerstdag. The presents, however, are modest in nature and

The wrapping seems to fascinate a toddler more than the gift inside on Eerste Kerstdag, or First Christmas Day.

On First Christmas Day, some Dutch families enjoy attending the ballet, such as a performance of the Dutch National Ballet's The Nutcracker.

totally without the diversion of the "surprises" that Sinterklaas brings. A carefully chosen book makes an appropriate gift.

In small provincial villages, this custom is less common. Solemn and conservative observances prevail. Some Dutch families, especially those in the south, believe in Father Christmas, called de Kerstman. He may bring gifts, just as he brings them to families in neighboring Germany and Belgium.

A day spent with family

Overall, however, the Dutch get their Christmas cheer from one another. The afternoon finds most homes welcoming relatives and close friends. People catch up on each other's news and play board games. Perhaps they listen to concerts, choral programs, and religious services aired on television especially for First Christmas Day. There are also concerts and ballets—including everyone's holiday favorite, *The Nutcracker*—to attend for those who prefer an outing.

Families may have reservations to dine at a restaurant. More than likely, however, the home kitchen is bustling with preparations for Christmas dinner.

During the course of the day, the family will sing and play Christmas carols around the tree. Favorite Dutch carols vary, but one that everyone knows is "Er Is een Kindeke Geboren" ("A Little

Child Is Born"). Others include carols famous the world over, especially "Silent Night."

To hold them over until dinner, the Dutch may nibble on a delicious sweet Christmas bread called kerstbrood or kerststol. Also made at Eastertime, this loaf is filled with raisins, currants, and candied fruit peel, then dusted with powdered sugar.

If the weather permits, and a hard frost has set in, the entire family may participate in a favorite pastime of the Dutch—ice skating.

From an early age, children learn to enjoy the ice.

Even the cooks leave the kitchen on First Christmas Day for a turn on the ice. The country's picturesque frozen ponds, lakes, rivers, and canals are filled with colorful skaters, like a scene from the paintings of the Dutch artists Bruegel or Avercamp. In the cities, many a town square is turned into an ice rink. Stalls selling hot chocolate, mulled wine, and an assortment of Christmas treats spring up around the rinks.

Everyone—from grandparents to small children—skates whenever possible. Those youngsters just learning push a chair along the ice in front of them. Families stay together by each hooking an arm over a long pole as they skate. Grownups even push baby carriages along the ice. Such antiques as sleighs and baby carriages with runners frequently make an appearance at Christmas.

Away from the large cities, age-old windmills line the shores of rivers and lakes, providing a quaint backdrop for the skaters. Of the 10,000 windmills that once dotted the countryside, about 1,000 remain, most dating from the 1700's and 1800's. East of Rotterdam, the town of Kinderdijk has 19 windmills.

The Christmas feast

Seven o'clock is the traditional time for the Christmas feast. The meal is abundant; the atmosphere, formal. Among many Dutch families, the custom is for either the oldest or the youngest person present to read the account of the Nativity from the Bible, echoing the reverent tone of the day.

The candlelit table draped in white linen may have a white or red poinsettia centerpiece. Holly and other greenery furnish additional decoration. Fresh irises or tulips, perhaps the gift of an appreciative guest, make the dinner table even more elegant.

The menu varies from family to family. It might begin with such appetizers as bitterballen, or cocktail meatballs, and zoute bolletjes, "salted bullets." The bitterballen are small croquettes of finely minced veal or beef in an herb-laced gelatin. They take some time to prepare, but adults especially enjoy them with an apéritif of Genever, the famous Dutch gin. The "bullets" are salty pastry dabs baked to a fine crunch.

Traditional favorites grace a Dutch table laden with the First Christmas Day feast.

A savory bowl of groentensoep, Dutch vegetable soup, or erwtensoep, the famous Dutch pea soup, may follow, sometimes served with little fried meatballs. The fish course may be mossel-rijstschotel, a delicious Indonesian-style casserole of mussels over cream-smothered rice. Indonesia, once a Dutch colony, has shown its influence on much of the Netherlands' cuisine. Or, the hosts may offer haringsla, herring salad. The Dutch love their

own special kind of herring, called matjes, for which the fish is gutted and salted at sea immediately after being caught, resulting in an especially tender fish.

Amsterdam's world-famous Royal Concertgebouw Orchestra traditionally gives a concert on Second Christmas Day.

The main course is usually rolled beef or game in the form of roast hare, goose, or venison. Turkey is a more modern choice that is gaining in popularity. Accompanying the meat, the Dutch enjoy potato puree, seasoned with any of a variety of spices and piped decoratively around the meat course.

Perhaps the most traditional Dutch Christmas dinner is served in a style called gourmetten. Using a table-top grill similar to a raclette grill, each guest cooks bite-sized pieces of meats and vegetables, much like diners make their own fondue.

As the table is cleared and coffee served, everyone still has room for a light dessert. That may be bessensappudding, a delicate, yet tart, currant pudding. Diners relish cookies and chocolates next, along with more coffee. Chocolate bells and wreaths are common, plain or topped with chopped nuts or sugary sprinkles.

Second Christmas Day

December 26, Second Christmas Day, is as sedate and refined as December 25 but not so home-centered. Many people call on friends and dine out. They also attend performances of all sorts. Churches, concert halls, and auditoriums throughout the country present choral, instrumental, and theatrical performances, both amateur and professional.

Children, led by teachers and Sunday school instructors, take part in choirs and Christmas plays in schools and churches. The plays usually depict the Nativity story, and each child takes a part. Not a character is forgotten. The children play the Holy Family, the Three Kings, the shepherds and angels—even the donkey that carried Mary. A baby brother or sister might portray the Infant Jesus.

Almost every Dutch community has an amateur choral group that performs on Second Christmas Day. Local brass bands or orchestras, ensembles, and professional vocalists provide audiences with an opportunity to hear yet again the inspiring carols of the season.

A tradition for many families in Rotterdam involves attending a performance of the Ahoy Kerstcircus (Christmas circus). The performance, which features a live band as well as aerial acts, animal acts, and clowns, has been an annual event during the Christmas season since 1917.

Exhibitions and festivals

A wide variety of exhibitions takes place throughout the country at this time of year. Schoolchildren have a holiday of several weeks at Christmastime, so the family often enjoys these days together when parents are also free. Kerstflora, for example, is a Christmas exhibition of bulb flowers that is held annually around the last week in December. It takes place at Hillegom, in the province of South Holland. Here, familiar flowers as well as some unusual varieties bloom in a myriad of colors.

Farther to the southeast, a snow and ice sculpture festival delights visitors. It was first held in the city of Eindhoven in the early 2000's and then moved to Roermond beginning in 2009. In late November, ice sculptors from throughout the world begin work on shimmering masterpieces that may include scenes from classic films or traditional stories and famous figures, both historic and imaginary. The festival takes place in a tent or building where the temperature is kept below freezing to preserve the elaborate sculptures. It is open until January of the new year.

And so, in ways special and different for every family, Christmas Days come to an end. But the spirit of Christmas, with all its traditions, beauty, and fellowship, endures for all.

ELFSTEDENTOCHT

For many children in the United States, the most exciting Dutch ice skating race was the one described by American author Mary Mapes Dodge in her book Hans Brinker, or, The Silver Skates. But for the Dutch today, the most anticipated ice skating race is one that has occurred barely over a dozen times in 100 years. That race is called the Elfstedentocht (Eleven Cities Tour), and each year, the Dutch eagerly await to learn whether this year conditions will be right for the race to be held once again.

The Elfstedentocht covers about 125 miles (200 kilometers) of ponds, canals, rivers, and lakes that connect 11 towns in Friesland, a northern province. It begins and ends in Leeuwaarden, the provincial capital. In order for the event to take place, the ice must be at least 6 inches (15 centimeters) thick throughout the length of the course. For the rivers and lakes to freeze to that thickness in all of Friesland, the winter must be very cold indeed. In general, the temperature in the entire area has to fall to 23 °F (-5 °C) or below and stay that low for about a week—unusual conditions—which is why the race has been held so infrequently.

Some historians trace the history of the Elfstedentocht to 1760. Others claim that it began in 1890, when a group of about 100 men and women challenged each other to skate along all of the cities in Friesland in one day. Everyone agrees, though, that the first official Elfstedentocht took place in 1909. Fifteen races were held in all from 1909 to 1997. In 1997, some 15,000 skaters participated, and an estimated 2 million people gathered to cheer them on. Having 15,000 people on the ice at one time is another reason that race organizers have to be very, very sure that the ice is completely frozen! But it is proof, once again, of how much the Dutch enjoy their traditional winter pastime.

Skaters race in the Elfstedentocht (Eleven Cities Tour) in Friesland in 1997, the last year temperatures were cold enough to properly freeze the course.

The haunting tones of hand-crafted horns echo
over the frozen landscape as part of an ancient
midwinter tradition.

Twelve Days of Christmas

The holiday spirit kindled by the Dutch in early November spills over into the Twelve Days of Christmas. When the merriment of Sinterklaas and the joy of Christmas end, there are still two more special occasions to enjoy: New Year's Eve and Three Kings' Day. Two winter activities also result in final contests—midwinter horn blowing and a bell-ringing custom called St. Thomasluiden.

From the first Sunday of Advent, which begins the Christmas season, to Three Kings' Day on January 6, people of the eastern, rural province of Overijssel hear strange tones sounding nightly in the distance. These are the sounds of midwinter horn blowing, called midwinter-hoornblazen. The origins of this Yuletide tradition are lost in time. Once believed to drive away evil spirits, the sound of the large, hand-crafted horns still haunts the frosty landscape.

The instruments have tremendous carrying power. On cold winter nights, across flat, wide-open farmland, people can hear the singular tone produced by one of these horns from nearly 2 miles (3 kilometers) away. Other horns from nearby farms answer with their own distinct note in a joint announcement of the coming birth of Christ.

The villages of Denekamp, Oldenzaal, and Ootmarsum, among others, continue this ancient custom. The horn makers start months in advance. Summer will find them carving the horn by hand from the limbs or trunks of birch, willow, alder, or poplar trees. Elderberry wood is used to make a mouthpiece.

The task is formidable. First, the horn maker must find a tree that contains a length of wood of suitable size and with a slightly curved shape. The trunk or branch is then sawed, planed, and chiseled. The piece is cut in half and hollowed out. When both the inside and the outside are as smooth as the horn maker can make them, the two halves are glued back together. The result is a horn that may be 3 ½ to 5 feet (1 to 1.5 meters) long.

Horns are made to be played either wet or dry. Each type produces a different sound. The length of the horn, its diameter, and the smoothness of the inside also affect the pitch of the tone the horn will produce. A wet horn is usually hung in a farmyard well during hornblowing season so that it would retain moisture and freeze inside. The smooth inside surface of a frozen horn makes a particularly pleasing tone. A frozen horn also becomes much heavier to hold. Often, horn blowers will rest the end of the horn on the edge of the well to support it.

Expert horn blowers are able to produce seven distinct tones with their horn. But achieving such proficiency requires a lot of practice, and playing a midwinter horn at any time of year other than Advent through Three Kings' Day is not allowed.

By the time people are sending their New Year's cards, final competitions in midwinter horn blowing are taking place. The champions will earn the respect of neighbors for the year—and perhaps the silver horn trophy. The winners often come together to perform unique compositions that can be heard daily through January 6.

The ancient art of St. Thomas ringing

Another age-old tradition that appears to be a relic of pagan custom is St. Thomasluiden, or St. Thomas ringing. This practice of continuous bell ringing takes place only at the klokkestoelen, or bellhouses, in the cemeteries of Friesland.

The custom may have been meant to dispel demons that lurked at year's end. Some link the tolling of the bells with the death of St. Thomas à Becket, venerated in Friesland as well as in England. Becket, the archbishop of Canterbury, was murdered in his cathedral on Dec. 29, 1170. His feast day is still celebrated on that day.

Today, the bells are rung in two Friesland villages, Katlijk and Oudehorne. Ringing the bells properly is a difficult art and usually involves two people dressed in traditional costume. Two bells—a large, heavy one and a small, light one—must be rung in harmony. When rung correctly, they produce a fascinating counterpoint.

St. Thomas ringing takes place from December 21 through December 31. Young and old try their hand at tolling the bells. Anyone from 16 to 21 years may compete in the championships.

Celebrating the Oude/Nieuw

New Year's Eve, which the Dutch call "Old Year's Evening," arrives amid great excitement all over the country. For the Dutch, this is a time for festive togetherness. They refer to December 31 and January 1 jointly as "Oude/Nieuw," or "Old/New." Most people want to be with their families, cheerfully celebrating the events of the two days.

In the late afternoon of December 31, streets

Bell ringers at a cemetery bellhouse continue the ancient Dutch tradition of continuous bell ringing from December 21 to December 31.

fill with workers rushing home from shops and offices. They call "Zalig Uiteinde!" to one another, meaning "Blessed End." The entire nation shuts down to celebrate the new year.

Many families attend church services early in the evening. Then the evening gives way to games and other amusements—and refreshments. As many generations of a family as possible attend. Even the young ones may stay up late to share the fun and welcome in the New Year.

A light supper is generally served around 11 o'clock. Usually it is a cold buffet of assorted delicacies, with pastries for dessert. Three treats that are favorites this time of year are made with apples. Appelbollen are whole apples that have been cored and then scrumptiously wrapped as buttery dumplings in puff pastry. With a cinnamon mixture inside, they are baked into golden balls. Appelflappen are batter-coated slices of apple that sizzle when taken from the deep fryer. The most popular and universal of all New Year's Eve refreshments are oliebollen. These crunchy doughnuts are loaded with currants and chunks of apple.

In the province of Limburg, merrymakers may bite into succulent wedges of Limburgse vlaai. A regional year-round favorite, the "Limburg pie" carries a healthy topping of fruit. In season, the fruit is baked fresh on the frothy dough. For New Year's, canned peaches or plums make good substitutes that all enjoy.

During the hour before midnight, television stations feature highlights of the previous year's news. The family stays tuned until

A line forms at an outdoor stand on New Year's Eve to sample freshly made oliebollen, crunchy doughnuts filled with currants and apples.

In a modern-day tradition, some brave and hearty souls plunge into the North Sea on New Year's Day.

about 11:45. Then, swallowing the last morsels of their New Year's treats, the youngsters run outside to prepare the fireworks, which are legal only on New Year's Eve.

The clock strikes 12:00 and the noise begins! Factories in the towns and ships in the harbors blast their whistles. Church bells peal and carillons play. Firecrackers explode on the ground and fireworks light up the sky.

Inside, there is a moment of thanksgiving. Then glasses clink and relatives embrace. They wish each other "Een Gelukkig Nieuwjaar!" or "Happy New Year!" Champagne, bishop's wine, or rum punch are served by the head of the household, who offers a toast to the coming year. Then the festivities move outside again as neighbor visits neighbor to offer good wishes for the New Year. The children finally go to bed, but most of the adults continue to celebrate into the wee hours.

New Year's Day

Because New Year's Day is a national holiday, most adults sleep late. The children, on the other hand, try to get up early. Each wants to be the first to greet relatives and friends with shouts of "Happy New Year" and to be rewarded with a shiny new coin. The remainder of the day, people continue their visits to friends and relatives. Somehow, everyone manages to find room for all the traditional cakes, fruit loaves, and pastries, which come out in force again this day.

At one time, freezing winter temperatures during the Twelve Days

of Christmas made the ice perfect for races and ice celebrations. But because the Dutch climate has become warmer in recent years, towns and cities have had to cancel many of these events. When the weather cooperates, however, costumed groups may still take celebrations to the frozen canals. Whole banquets have been served there on the island of Marken, off the east coast of North Holland, followed by dancing and skating.

In modern times, it has become a tradition in dozens of communities to begin the new year with a bracing dive into freezing water. One of the most popular places to take the leap is Scheveningen, a suburb of The Hague in South Holland. There, at noon on January 1, some 10,000 people dive off the pier into the North Sea. A nice hot cup of pea soup hits the spot after a hasty retreat!

Three Kings' Day

January 6, the feast of the Epiphany, is known as Driekoningendag, or Three Kings' Day. The young are generally the focus of the activities on this day. An Epiphany cake with a bean or almond baked inside is the center of attention. Sometimes this cake is a tulband, which is similar to Christmas bread, only baked in a bundt pan. Whoever finds the bean or nut in his or her piece of cake becomes monarch for the day. A gold paper crown sets the lucky one apart from the courtiers.

There is another Three Kings' Day custom in the predominantly Roman Catholic provinces of North Brabant and Limburg. The children dress as the Three Kings, as shepherds, or as angels. Then they parade through the streets of their neighborhoods carrying candles or homemade stars and Chinese lanterns. They sing Epiphany songs as they march along. Often, they will go from house to house, where they receive treats.

Three Kings' Day marks the official end of the winter holiday season. On January 6, families take down the Christmas tree and all the decorations, if they have not already done so.

Many Dutch towns hold an organized burning of Christmas trees. Local firefighters are always on hand to keep the activities in order. The match is struck, and the trees go up in a blaze, ending another Christmas season.

Fireworks light up the sky behind a windmill during a New Year's Eve celebration in Amsterdam.

The Magi present their gifts to the Christ Child in the painting The Adoration of the Kings *(1564) by Pieter Bruegel the Elder.*

Christmas theme in Dutch art

The Dutch are known for a style of art known as genre painting that was especially popular in the 1600's. Dutch genre painters captured the daily life of the peasant and middle classes in a straightforward way, in minute detail. Pieter Bruegel the Elder (1525?-1569) was one of the earliest masters of the tradition. Jan Steen (1626?-1679) became one of the style's most gifted practitioners. And hundreds of other Dutch genre painters—using a facial expression, a body posture, a tool, or a toy—faithfully recorded how the people of their time lived, worked, and celebrated the most important moments of their lives, including such religious holidays as Christmas. Take a close look at the paintings on this page and pages 60 and 61—and then look again—to discover the rich details hidden in each winter scene.

In The Census at Bethlehem *(1566) by Pieter Bruegel the Elder, Mary and Joseph (center front) appear in a scene depicting the routines of daily life among the common people of Bruegel's day.*

In The Feast of St. Nicholas *(c. 1663-1665, above), Jan Steen immortalizes a family on a favorite Dutch holiday. A boy cries, having found a switch in his shoe, while his sister rejoices over a new doll and a bucketful of sweets; his little brother gloats with a new golf club and balls. But why is grandmother (in the background, opening a curtain) smiling as she beckons him?*

Neighbors chat, children skate, and fishermen prepare to cut a hole in the ice in Jan van Goyen's (1596-1656) Winter Landscape with a Walled Castle *(1626, opposite page).*

In Steen's Twelfth Night (1668, above), a family celebrates the last day of the Christmas season amid much laughter and revelry. A child (wearing paper crown) has found the bean hidden in the Epiphany cake and is treated to a "coronation" drink. At right, a man plays a rommelpot, a traditional Dutch instrument.

Dutch Recipes

Speculaas *(St. Nicholas cookies)*

1 cup softened, unsalted butter
2 tsp. vanilla
1 cup white sugar
1¼ cups dark brown sugar,
   firmly packed
2 large, beaten eggs
3½ cups all-purpose flour
2 tsp. baking soda

2 tsp. cinnamon
1 tsp. nutmeg
1 tsp. ground cloves
½ tsp. ginger
½ tsp. ground anise seed
⅛ tsp. salt

1. Combine butter and vanilla with the white and brown sugars and beat until light and fluffy. Add beaten eggs and blend well.

2. Sift the flour and all remaining dry ingredients together and beat into butter mixture.

3. At this point you may do several things:

   Form cookies by rolling small pieces of dough into balls and baking on a greased cookie sheet for 10-15 minutes in a 350 °F oven.

   Or, divide the dough into 2 equal rolls about 2½ inches in diameter, wrap well, and chill for several hours or overnight. After chilling, either cut the rolls into ⅛-inch to ¼-inch slices, place on greased cookie sheets about ½ inch apart, or roll the cooled dough out to ⅛-inch to ¼-inch thickness and use cookie cutters.

4. Bake at 350 °F for 10-15 minutes.

Yield: about 60 small cookies

Pepernoten *(spicy cookie balls)*

2 cups all-purpose flour
½ tsp. baking powder
¼ tsp. cinnamon
¼ tsp. nutmeg
¼ tsp. ground anise seed

¼ tsp. ground cloves
1¼ cups dark brown sugar, firmly
   packed
2 large eggs
1 Tbsp. diced candied orange rind

1. Sift flour with baking powder and spices. Add remaining ingredients and combine until mixture forms a dough.

2. With floured hands, form the dough into about 60 ½-inch balls and place on greased cookie sheets. Bake at 350 °F for 15-20 minutes, or until they are light brown. Store in an airtight container.

Yield: 60 small cookies

Oliebollen *(apple-raisin doughnuts)*

1 cup milk	1 egg
1 Tbsp. sugar	3 cups all-purpose flour
2 Tbsp. unsalted butter	2 cups chopped, tart apples
½ tsp. salt	¾ cup dried currants or raisins
1 package dry yeast	oil for deep frying
½ cup very warm water	powdered sugar

1. Heat milk, sugar, butter, and salt just until warm. Dissolve yeast in warm water and add milk mixture, egg, and 1½ cups of flour. Beat until smooth.

2. Stir in apples and currants or raisins and add remaining flour to form a soft dough. Cover and let rise in a warm place until doubled in bulk, about 1 hour.

3. Drop tablespoon by tablespoon, a few at a time, into oil that has been heated to 375 °F. Fry until golden brown, about 5 minutes.

4. Drain on paper towels and roll in powdered sugar.

Yield: about 30 fritters

Sneeuwballen *(snowballs)*

½ cup water	2 large eggs
¼ cup unsalted butter	2 Tbsp. dried currants or raisins
⅛ tsp. salt	2 Tbsp. diced candied fruits or
¼ tsp. sugar	peels
½ cup all-purpose flour	oil for deep frying

1. Combine water, butter, salt, and sugar in a small, deep saucepan and bring to a boil. Boil gently until all the ingredients have melted. Remove from the heat. Add the flour all at once and mix rapidly with a wooden spoon to a smooth paste.

2. Add eggs one at a time, beating thoroughly after each addition. Add currants or raisins and candied fruits.

3. Heat oil to 375 °F and, with a metal spoon that should be dipped in the hot oil, drop the dough by spoonfuls into the oil. Fry 5-8 minutes, or until puffed up and golden brown.

4. Drain on paper towels and dust with powdered sugar.

Yield: 8 large or 16 small snowballs

Banketletters *(almond-filled pastries)*

Dough:
1 cup very cold unsalted butter (no substitutes)
2 cups all-purpose flour
½ cup cold sour cream
1 large, beaten egg yolk

1. Cut butter into small pieces and add to flour. Using a pastry blender or 2 knives, cut the butter into the flour until the butter is the size of peas. Mix sour cream with the egg yolk and blend into flour/butter mixture with a fork just until the dough forms a ball.

2. Divide the dough into 2 pieces, wrap well, and refrigerate for several hours or days, if desired. Allow dough to come to room temperature before making cookies.

Filling:
1 8-oz. can almond paste or, to make your own:
¼ lb. blanched almonds
½ cup granulated sugar
1 large, beaten egg

3. Grind the almonds and mix with the sugar. Add the egg and, using a wooden spoon or your hands, work until smooth. The almond paste will keep for several weeks if wrapped well and refrigerated.

4. Roll the dough out to ⅛-inch thickness and cut dough into strips 3½ to 4 inches wide.

5. Work the almond paste into little round sticks about the length and diameter of your finger. Lay these almond paste sticks either end to end for a long cookie that may be formed into a wreath or crosswise to roll the dough around each stick individually. For sticks, cut the dough, place a dab of water under each end, and tuck under. Begin again with the next "stick." Sticks may also be formed into initials by making slits where parts of letters must join and dampening with a little water.

6. Place cookies, initials, or wreath seam side down on a cookie sheet and brush with 1 egg that has been beaten with 1 Tbsp. of water. Bake at 400 °F for 20-25 minutes or until golden brown. Cool on a rack. May be served warm if desired.

Yield: about 20 cookies

Appelflappen *(apple fritters)*

Fritter batter:
1 cup all-purpose flour
½ tsp. salt
1 Tbsp. corn oil
½ cup water or milk
2 egg whites, stiffly beaten
oil for deep frying
powdered sugar

1. Sift flour and salt into a bowl. Make a well in the center and add oil and water or milk, beating until smooth. Allow to rest for 45 minutes to an hour.

2. Fold in the beaten eggs whites with a rubber spatula.

Apples:
4 to 5 tart apples
1 cup light brown sugar, firmly packed
1 Tbsp. cinnamon
1 tsp. nutmeg

3. Peel and core apples and slice into ¼-inch to ½-inch rings.

4. Coat with sugar that has been mixed with the cinnamon and nutmeg.

5. Heat cooking oil to 375 °F. Dip coated apple slice into fritter batter and fry in hot oil. Turn several times until both sides are golden brown.

6. Drain on paper towels and sift with powdered sugar.

Yield: 4-6 servings.

Bessensappudding (*currant pudding*)

4 eggs, separated
1 cup crushed currant juice and
 ½ cup brown, firmly packed sugar *or* substitute
 1 cup frozen, concentrated cranberry cocktail juice,
 omitting all or part of the sugar
1 envelope unflavored gelatin, softened in ¼ cup water

1. Stir yolks (and sugar) till thick and foamy. Add juice and heat mixture on low flame until somewhat thickened and the foam has mostly disappeared.

2. Dissolve softened gelatin in this mixture. Fold in beaten egg whites and cool, stirring occasionally until egg whites and custard no longer separate.

3. Pour into pudding mold rinsed with egg white or oil. Chill and unmold. Serve topped with sweetened whipped cream and with wafers or ladyfingers. Yield: 6 servings

Borstplaat (*fondants*)

1 cup sugar
3 Tbsp. liquid (water, milk, half and half,
 or light cream)
1 tsp. butter
a few drops of flavoring or extract
a few drops of food coloring

1. In a small, heavy saucepan, mix the sugar and liquid. Heat slowly to a boil without stirring until the syrup registers 240 °F on a candy thermometer.

2. Remove from heat immediately and add the butter, flavoring, and food coloring.

3. Stir vigorously until mixture thickens. Either drop from a spoon onto waxed paper or pour into greased lids no more than ⅓-inch high. Cool to solidify.

Variations:

For *fruit-flavored borstplaat*, add fruit or flavoring and appropriate food coloring.

For *coffee-flavored borstplaat*, the 3 Tbsp. of liquid should consist of 1½ Tbsp. strong coffee and 1½ Tbsp. half and half or light cream.

For *chocolate-flavored borstplaat*, add 2 Tbsp. unsweetened cocoa powder to the sugar and use 3 Tbsp. half and half or light cream for the liquid. Stir to dissolve any lumps before heating.

Yield: 12 medium candies.

Kerstbrood *(Christmas bread)*

2 packages dry yeast
¼ cup very warm water
¾ cup milk at room temperature or slightly warmed
½ cup sugar
½ tsp. salt
½ cup softened, unsalted butter
3 large, lightly beaten eggs, reserving 1 egg white
1 cup raisins or currants, or a mixture of both
½ cup diced citron
½ cup diced orange peel or candied fruit
4¼ cups all-purpose flour
¾ cup chopped, blanched almonds
2 tsp. cinnamon
½ cup powdered sugar for dusting

1. Mix the yeast with the water and stir to dissolve. Add the milk, sugar, salt, butter, and 2 whole eggs plus the yolk from the third egg. Blend well.

2. In a separate bowl, dust the raisins, currants, citron, and orange peel or candied fruit with a little of the flour and the cinnamon, and then add the almonds.

3. Add half the flour to the yeast mixture and stir until smooth. Cover and let rise in a warm place until doubled in bulk, about 1 hour. This mixture is called a sponge.

4. Add the remaining flour and knead until smooth and elastic, about 5 minutes. Knead in the fruits and nuts.

5. Place the dough in an oiled bowl, turning the dough so it is completely coated. Cover and let rise for about 30 minutes.

6. Divide the dough into 2 equal portions and press each dough ball into a large, flat circle. Fold each circle over so the top half is 1 inch from the edge of the bottom half, forming a split-loaf shape.

7. Place on a greased baking sheet, cover with plastic wrap, and let rise again until doubled in size, about 30 minutes.

8. Bake at 375 °F for 40 minutes until golden brown. Cool on wire rack and sprinkle top generously with powdered sugar before serving.

Yield: 2 loaves, or about 20 servings

Appelbollen (apple dumplings)

Dough: As for *banketletters*, page 64.

Apples:
6 tart apples
½ cup light brown sugar, firmly packed
1½ tsp. cinnamon
1 egg, beaten

1. Peel and core apples. Mix brown sugar with cinnamon and fill each apple with about 2 Tbsp. of mixture.

2. Roll dough out to about ⅛-inch thickness. Cut the dough into squares large enough to enclose the apples.

3. Place apples topside down on each square of dough and wrap the dough around the apple, corner to corner. Moisten the dough edges with a little water to seal and then press edges together. Prepare each apple in the same way.

4. Arrange the dumplings, seam side down, in a buttered baking dish. Brush each one with a mixture of 1 egg beaten with 1 Tbsp. water.

5. Bake at 425 °F for 10 minutes and then 45 minutes more at 350 °F. Dumplings are done when the crust is golden brown and the apples are cooked through.

Yield: 6 apple dumplings

Slemp (slemp)

2 cinnamon sticks
12 whole cloves
1 tsp. loose black tea leaves
⅛ tsp. ground nutmeg
¼ tsp. ground mace
pinch saffron
cheesecloth
cooking twine
4 cups whole milk
2-inch strip lemon peel,
   bitter white pith removed
¼ cup sugar
1 tbsp. cornstarch

1. Place the first 6 ingredients on a square of cheesecloth and tie tightly with cooking twine. Place milk and bag of spices in a medium saucepan. Warm over low heat until barely simmering. Lower heat and cook for 30 minutes. Remove spice bag. Add sugar; stir until dissolved.

2. Dissolve cornstarch in 1 Tbsp. cold water. Add to milk mixture. Stir until slightly thickened.

Yield: 4 servings

Kerstkrans (*Christmas fruitcake ring*)

5 oz. blanched almonds
5 oz. powdered sugar
1 tsp. vanilla extract
1 egg
peel of 1 lemon
1 portion puff pastry, made from
   ½ cup very cold, unsalted butter;
   1 cup flour;
   ¼ cup cold sour cream;
   and 1 small, beaten egg yolk

5 candied cherries
1 beaten egg
apricot preserves
thin lemon icing

1. Filling (make up to 1 month in advance): Grind almonds with sugar in grinder or blender. Add vanilla, egg, and lemon peel, mix well, and grind again.

2. Puff pastry: Cut butter into small pieces and add to flour. Cut butter into flour until butter is size of peas. Mix sour cream with egg yolk and blend into flour/butter mixture with fork just until dough forms a ball. Wrap well and refrigerate for several hours at least. Allow dough to come to room temperature. Roll out into a long strip, ⅛-inch thick, 4 inches wide.

3. Shape almond paste into a roll, about 1-inch thick and of nearly the same length as the dough. Press 10 halved cherries at equal intervals into roll. Reshape.

4. Place roll on dough, a little above center. Wet lower part of dough and wrap loosely around roll. Do not let dough overlap more than enough to seal edges. Place roll, seam down, on baking sheet as you shape roll into a ring. Join ends with water. Brush with egg. Heat oven to 450 °F. Place ring in refrigerator for 15 minutes. Then bake 20 minutes until golden brown.

5. Coat ring thinly with preserves and, while still hot, with thin icing (made with powdered sugar and a few drops of water and lemon juice). Cool on baking sheet.

6. When firm, carefully lift and cool on wire rack. Decorate with halved candied cherries, orange peel, lemon peel, ribbon, and holly.

Yield: 10-12 small pieces

Dutch Crafts

Pinwheel ornament

1. Cut two 6-inch squares from the foil, one of each color, and work both pieces together, foil sides out. Use a dab of white glue between the points and in the center to hold the squares together.

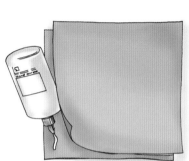

2. Cut a diagonal line from each corner to 1 inch from center.

3. Take every other point and bend over center. Using a nail or a hole punch, carefully make a small hole through the points at center. Push paper fastener through the hole from the front. Open paper fastener at back of pinwheel.

4. Attach pipe cleaner to back of fastener. Hang ornament from tree with pipe cleaner. Repeat for more pinwheels.

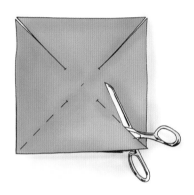

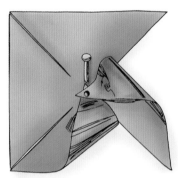

Materials

- 2 colors foil paper (gift-wrap is suitable), to be glued paper side to paper side with foil sides out
- scissors
- ruler
- hole punch (a nail will also work)
- 1-inch brass paper fasteners
- 9-inch colored pipe cleaners
- white glue

If desired, multicolored pinwheels or patterned pinwheels may be made from several different foil combinations. You can also use a 12-inch square to make a pinwheel ornament for the top of the tree or to use as a decoration elsewhere.

Painted walnuts

1. Ask an adult to help you crack each walnut into two unbroken halves, using a nutcracker or butter knife. Remove the nutmeats and set aside for baking or eating.

2. Cut a 6-inch piece of wire. Twist the ends together to form a loop. Tuck twisted end of loop into end of one walnut-shell half. Put a thin coat of glue on the edge of the other walnut-shell half and fit the two halves back together. Dry thoroughly. Repeat for each walnut.

3. On a level surface, set wire cooling rack on top of glasses, one glass at each corner.

4. Holding a walnut by wire, paint desired color. With ornament hanger or string, suspend walnut from wire rack to dry. Repeat with other walnuts, arranging them on rack so weight of ornaments is evenly distributed.

5. When completely dry, hang walnuts from tree.

Materials

- walnuts in the shell
- hinge-type nutcracker or butter knife
- beading wire, or very thin wire
- scissors
- white glue
- wire cooling rack
- 4 tall glasses of equal height
- nontoxic tempera poster paints
- small paint brushes
- ornament hangers or string

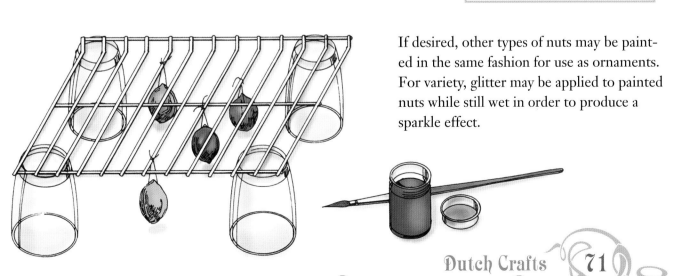

If desired, other types of nuts may be painted in the same fashion for use as ornaments. For variety, glitter may be applied to painted nuts while still wet in order to produce a sparkle effect.

Kerstkransjes
(Christmas wreath cookies)

Ingredients

- ⅔ cup butter
- ½ cup honey
- 1 Tbsp. water
- 2¼ cups whole wheat pastry flour *or;* substitute 2½ cups all-purpose flour
- 1 tsp. baking powder
- finely grated peel of ½ lemon
- 1 egg, beaten
- rock sugar *or;* substitute colored sugar crystals
- ½ cup chopped, blanched almonds
- extra flour and butter

Materials

- measuring cups and spoons
- rubber spatula
- 1 large and 1 small mixing bowl
- electric or hand mixer
- mixing spoon
- plastic food wrap
- pastry board
- rolling pin
- drinking glass with rim 1½ inches to 3 inches in diameter
- cookie sheets
- thimble
- knife or nut chopper
- pastry brush
- potholders
- wire cooling rack
- 18-inch lengths of thin, red ribbon

1. Bring all ingredients to room temperature. In large mixing bowl, cream butter, honey, and water together with mixer until well blended.

2. With spoon, mix flour, baking powder, and lemon peel together in small mixing bowl. Add a little at a time to butter/honey mixture, mixing continually. Knead until mixture forms a soft ball, adding more flour, if necessary. Chill dough in food wrap for at least 1 hour.

For 2-inch cookies:

3. Preheat oven to 375 °F. On floured board, roll half the dough out to ⅛-inch thickness. Cut out circles with glass. Cut out centers with thimble to create cookie wreaths. Reserve centers to make more cookies.

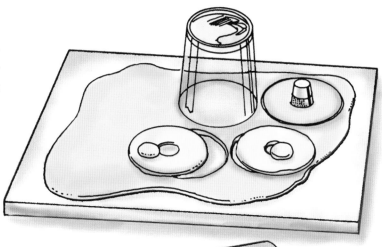

4. Place cookies on buttered cookie sheet, about 1 inch apart. Lightly brush cookies with beaten egg and sprinkle with sugar and chopped almonds. Bake cookies for about 8 minutes, or until golden brown. (Length of cooking will increase and decrease with size of cookie desired.) Begin preparing second half of dough while first batch bakes. Remove cookies from oven and cool on sheet until no longer soft. Remove to wire rack to cool completely.

5. Tie the cooled cookies to the tree with lengths of red ribbon, one length for each cookie. Children may remove wreath cookies from tree as Christmas treats.

Yield: about 6 dozen 2-inch cookie wreaths

Dutch Carols

Bright December Moon
(Zie de Maan Schijnt)

Andante

Traditional

Bright De - cem-ber moon is beam— ing. Boys and girls now stop your play! For to-
Zie de maan schijnt door de bo— men, Mak-kers staakt uw wild ge-raas! 't Heerlijk

night's the wondrous eve - ning, Eve of good St. Nicholas Day. O'er the
a - vondj' is ge- ko- men, 't A-vond - je van Sin - ter klaas. Vol ver-

roofs his horse un- shod, Brings us gifts or else the rod.
wach - ting klopt ons hart, Wie de koek krijgt wie de gard.

O'er the roofs his horse un- shod, Brings us gifts or else the rod.
Vol ver-wach - ting klopt ons hart, Wie de koek krijgt wie de gard.

The snow-covered harbor at Leiden, in South Holland, is bathed in moonlight on a late-December evening.

Look, There Is the Steamer

Adagio

(Zie Ginds Komt de Stoomboot)

Traditional

1. Look, there is the steam-er from far-a-way lands. It
Zie ginds komt de stoom-boot uit Span-je weer aan. Hij

brings us St. Nich'las, he's waving his hands. His horse is a - pranc-ing on
brengt ons Sint Niklaas, ik zie hem al staan. Hoe hup - pelt zijn paard - je het

deck, up and down, The ban-ners are wa-ving in vil-lage and town.
dek op en neer, Hoe waai-en de wim-pels al heen en al weer.

2. Black Peter is laughing And tells everyone,
"The good kids get candy, The bad kids get none!"
Oh, please, dear St. Nicholas, If Pete and you would,
Just visit our house For we all have been good.

Good Saint Nicholas

(Sint Niklaasje Kom Maar Binnen)

Allegretto   Traditional

Good St. Nich'las is in Holland once a-gain With his horse and Peter from
Sint Ni - klaasje kom maar bin-nen met je knecht, En we zit- ten al - le-maal

sun - ny Spain. And e - ven if he can't stay long, We hope he'll
e - ven recht, Mis - schièn heeft u wel e - ven tijd, Voor u

stop to hear our song. Dear St. Ni - cho-las the door is o-pen
weer naar Span - je rijdt. Sint Ni - klaasje kom maar e - ven bij ons

wide, For you and Pete to step in- side. And we're singing, voices
aan, Maar laat uw schim- mel bui- ten staan. En we zin-gen en we

ringing, and our hearts re - joice 'Cause the saint loves all good girls and boys.
springen en we zijn zo blij, Want er zijn geen stou- te kind'- ren bij.

Nicholas, I Beg of You
(Sinterklaas Kapoentje)

Moderato   Traditional

Ni - cho - las, I   beg of   you,   Drop in - to   my   little   shoe,
Sin-ter-klaas, Ka - poen -   tje,   Gooi   wat   in   mijn   schoen- tje,

Something sweet or   sweet - er,   Thank you, Saint   and   Pe - ter.
Gooi   wat   in   mijn   laars - je,   Dank   U,   Sin - ter -   klaas - je.

Sinterklaas and Pete arrive in Holland.

A Little Child Is Born

(Er Is een Kindeke Geboren)

Andante con moto

Traditional

1. From Heav'n there came to earth a Ba - by so small: From
1. Er is een Kin - de - ke ge - bo - ren op aard': Er-

Heav'n there came to earth a Ba - by so small:
is een Kin - de - ke ge - bo - ren op aard':

Je - sus, who came for the sake of us all.
't Kwam op de aar - de voor ons al - le - gaar.

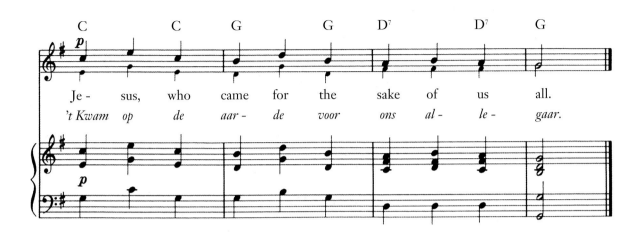

Je - sus, who came for the sake of us all.
'*t Kwam op de aar - de voor ons al - le - gaar.*

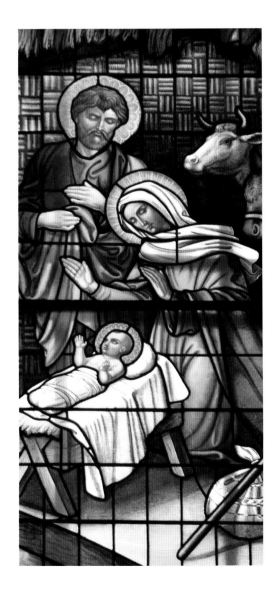

2. Beneath his tiny head no pillow but hay,
   God's richest treasure in rude manger lay.

3. His eyes of blackest jet were sparkling with light,
   Rosy cheeks bloomed on his face fair and bright.

4. And from his lovely mouth, the laughter did swell,
   When he saw Mary, whom he loved so well.

5. He came to weary earth, so dark and so drear,
   To wish to mankind a blessed New Year.

*A stained glass window in St. Nicholas
Church in Amsterdam features a
Nativity scene.*

Acknowledgments

The publishers gratefully acknowledge the following sources for photography. All illustrations and maps were prepared by WORLD BOOK unless otherwise noted.

Cover: © Floris Leeuwenberg, Corbis; © Shutterstock
2: © Richard Wareham Fotografie/Alamy Images
5: © iStockphoto
6: © Peter Dejong, AP Images
8: © Eric Minnaard, www.sintinamsterdam.nl; © Frans Lemmens, The Image Bank/Getty Images
10: © Eric Minnaard, www.sintinamsterdam.nl
11: © Hanne Nijhuis, www.sintinamsterdam.nl
12: © JTB Photo Communications, Inc./ Alamy Images
13: © Hanne Nijhuis, www.sintinamsterdam.nl; © Jolanda van der Linden, www.sintinamsterdam.nl
14: © Claude Levesque (Entreprise Int. de Photographie)
16: © Bjorn Svensson, Alamy Images
17: © Eric Minnaard, www.sintinamsterdam.nl; © Shanni Lim Shang Nee, Getty Images
18: © Dreamstime
19: © Nicole Holten, www.thedutchtable.com
20: © Owen Franken, Corbis; © Stuart Forster, Alamy Images
21: WORLD BOOK photo by Steve Hale; Bedrijf-schap Banketbakkersbedrijf; © Shutterstock
22: © Catchlight Visual Services/Alamy Images; © Nicole Holten, www.thedutchtable.com; © Shutterstock
23: © Shutterstock
24: © Frans Lemmens, Alamy Images
25: © Rex USA
26: © Dreamstime
28: © Bas Czerwinski, AP Photo
29: © Shutterstock
30: © Catchlight Visual Services/Alamy Images
31: Verkeersburo Stichting VVV Friesland-Leeuwarden
33: © David R. Gee, Alamy Images; © Maartje Blijdenstein, AFP/Getty Images
34: © Valerie Kuypers, AFP/Getty Images
35: © Fred Ernst, AP Images
36: © Shutterstock
37: © Prisma Bildagentur AG/Alamy Images; © Shutterstock
38: © Marc van Woudenberg, www.amsterdamize.com
39: © Spaarnestad B.V.
41: © Shutterstock

43: © Shutterstock; © Dreamstime
44: © Richard Wareham Fotografie/ Alamy Images
45: © Catchlight Visual Services/Alamy Images
46: © Angela Sterling, Het National Ballet
47: © Buiten-Beeld/Alamy Images; © iStockphoto
48: © Bon Appetit/Alamy Images
49: Wladimir Polak, Lebrecht Music and Arts Photo Library
51: © Frans Lemmens, SuperStock
52: © Hans Hendriksen
54: Frisian Tourist Office VVV
55: © Lex Van Lieshout, AFP/Getty Images; © Nicole Holten, www.thedutchtable.com
56: © Dreamstime
57: © Richard Wareham Fotografie/ Alamy Images
58: © National Gallery, London/Art Resource
59: © Scala/Art Resource
60: Rijksmuseum, Amsterdam
61: © Erich Lessing, Art Resource; © Guildhall Art Gallery, City of London/Harold Samuel Collection/The Bridgeman Art Library
62: © Dreamstime
63: © Nicole Holten, www.thedutchtable.com
64: WORLD BOOK photo by Steve Hale
65: WORLD BOOK photo by Steve Hale
66: © Nicole Holten, www.thedutchtable.com
67: © Nicole Holten, www.thedutchtable.com
68: © Nicole Holten, www.thedutchtable.com
74: © Dreamstime
77: © Shutterstock
79: © iStockphoto

Craft Illustrations:
James M. Curran, Brenda Tropinski
Advent Calendar:
© Lebrecht Music and Arts Photo Library/Alamy Images
Advent calendar and recipe card illustrations:
Eileen Mueller Neill
Recipe consultant and recipe card editor:
Karen Zack Ingebretsen